Going the Distance:
A Handbook for
Part-Time & Adjunct
Faculty Who Teach Online

Revised First Edition
Evelyn Beck and Donald Greive, Ed.D.

Order information:

To order copies of this book, please contact Part-Time Press, at P.O. Box 130117, Ann Arbor, Michigan 48113-0117. The phone number is 734-930-6854. Orders may be faxed to: 734-665-9001.

First printing: April, 2005
Revised: May, 2008

Copyright 2008, *Part-Time Press, Inc.*

ISBN-10: 0-940017-02-4 (paperback)
ISBN-13: 978-0-940017-02-3 (paperback)

Printed in the United States of America.

INTRODUCTION

Enrollment boom

Distance education saw the earliest widespread use in institutions in Europe and Australia. Its beginnings can be traced back in the United States through correspondence courses and then instructional television, which expanded its range with the advent of satellite technology. The end of the Cold War, coupled with the spread of Internet access in the 1990s, has led to a global-wide embrace of online learning by both non-profit, as well as for profit colleges and universities.

In 2007, over three million students were enrolled in online courses at U.S. colleges and universities. This figure represents nearly 20 percent of the nation's 17.5 million college students, according to the National Center for Education Statistics. By Fall 2011, the USDLA estimates that the majority of university students will have participated in at least one online course at some point during their college careers. Distance education has reached every corner of the Academy, from exclusive Ivy League schools, to rural community colleges. Eighty-one percent of all higher education institutions offer at least one course that is either fully or partly online, and 34 percent offer entire online degree programs. Most college officials believe that distance education is an important element in their future plans, and more and more faculty are coming to agree that online classes are at least as effective as face-to-face classes in helping students to master the material. Online higher education has even become a recruiting tool for the armed services, evidenced by successful ventures such as eArmyU and the Air Force Institute for Distance Learning.

Hybrid courses

If you live near the college where you've been hired to teach online, you may one day find yourself asked to teach a hybrid course, which combines the best features of traditional education with the advantages of technology. Increasingly popular, these courses are part online, part face-to-face and offer students the flexibility of Internet instruction along with the personalized support of classroom interaction.

For example, in a hybrid economics course at Randolph Community College in Pinehurst, N.C., students access information and take tests online, then meet once a week for supplemental support. Class time for the instructor involves answering questions from the previous week's material, reviewing economic principles, and giving a mini-lecture on new material for the following week. Other instructors of hybrid courses use class time for tutoring or lab work.

Some studies suggest better student success rates with hybrid courses, perhaps because such courses demand more involvement from students. In a well-designed hybrid, students must interact with peers online, then attend class and face the instructor and their classmates. These dual environments present more kinds of stimulus, from in-class group problem solving and lectures to online simulations and discussion boards.

Hybrid courses do have drawbacks. For example, there's the potential for class time to be consumed by technological questions unrelated to course material, a problem that can be solved by anticipating students' technology questions at the outset and providing help in advance. And hybrid courses certainly aren't feasible for students who seek distance education because they can't come to campus.

The employer perspective

How do employers judge the value of the courses you're teaching online? What do they think of candidates whose degrees were earned via the Internet? The results of a number of recent studies are mixed, with many business professionals uneasy about the quality of online learning, but with a majority of academics convinced that Web courses are just as effective as classroom-based education.

A September 2000 survey of 239 human resource professionals by Vault.com, a career resources firm based in New York City, found that HR professionals are extremely skeptical about degrees earned wholly through distance learning. Only 26 percent of those surveyed by Vault.com believed that an online undergraduate degree was as good as one earned by attending classes on campus, particularly if the degree came from a virtual university. More than half of those surveyed felt that online degrees were simply too new to judge effectively, and they voiced concerns about degrees earned through online study. Those concerns included lower academic standards on the part of the college or university granting the degree. In addition, those surveyed feared students educated in distance education programs would be less able to think critically. Finally, the HR professionals surveyed were particularly concerned about the fact that students in online learning programs have minimal face-to-face interaction with faculty and with other students.

While diplomas do not make a distinction between degrees earned online or on campus, such a distinction might be revealed during the interview process. The Vault.com survey found that some fields are more open to online degree-holders than others. Not surprisingly, technology and Internet businesses were more likely than other firms to hire graduates who had earned their degrees online. In contrast, a 2000 *Business Week* survey of 247 companies found that most "hadn't considered hiring an MBA with an online degree."

Truth be told, acceptance of degrees earned online is probably inevitable as more employers take advantage of online courses as a less disruptive form of workforce training. Added to that, there are studies of distance education student achievement which recognize the viability of distance education. For instance, Thomas Russell, who's been running distance education programs in many forms at North Carolina State University for forty years, discovered through a study he conducted that students in online courses are succeeding at the same rates as their in-class counterparts. Looking at 355 distance education courses and comparing them to traditional classroom student outcomes, he found that "the research says there's no significant difference using traditional measurement standards. Tests average about the same or slightly higher grades from online students."

What does all of this mean for you, the part-time faculty member who teaches online courses? First of all, as colleges expand their distance education offerings, they rely increasingly on you, their adjunct faculty, to teach these courses. Because of the nature of this medium, colleges are able to expand instructor pools to include those who live off campus and even out of state. While this flexibility is appealing for both the institution and the adjunct, it also creates challenges for the instructor.

Unfortunately, even if you live in the same town as the college that employs you to teach online, you may find yourself assigned a course with little direction and with insufficient access to your institution's instructional and/or technical resources. Part-time faculty who teach distance education courses need mentoring and reliable support.

Going the Distance: A Handbook for Part-Time & Adjunct Faculty Who Teach Online provides the part-time and adjunct faculty who read it with the much-needed mentoring and support they need to be successful distance educators. Readers learn what questions to ask, how to select and compile materials, as well as how to plan their courses so as to successfully deliver courses at a distance. Finally, *A Handbook for Part-Time & Adjunct Faculty Who Teach Online* helps part- time faculty members develop the confidence and teaching skills necessary to make certain that their students succeed in the online classroom, as well.

Evelyn Beck

CONTENTS

Resources

Table of Figures

Chapter One

Getting Started

So, your teaching schedule calls for you to teach a distance education course. It doesn't matter if this is your first such venture, or you have taught at a distance before—it should be approached as if it were your first ever. Recall that when you decided to enter the teaching profession, you looked to the human interaction with students as a major factor in your decision. You were to be the conductor, and every class a symphony with lots of direction and emotion involved in the production (class). Now you are about to enter a new arena. As such, you must view yourself as an engineer on a train. The train has many cars—each is loaded with different course delivery technologies which you will need to call upon to reach your destination (objectives). The goods you must deliver, the students, are in the last car. Sometimes, you can't even see them.

This book will provide you the skills necessary to complete your journey—through the use of technology. However, as with teaching face-to-face, preparation is necessary. In fact, perhaps it's even slightly more important. In a classroom, it is easy to recover from a mishap or an error; in a distance learning situation, it is much more difficult. There are two major factors that you must keep in mind while preparing for your distance education courses: you *must have* complete command of the technology, and you must not lose sight of the fact that the human touch alluded to earlier is not de-emphasized, but is, in fact, emphasized as much as possible.

Master the technology, but do not get so wrapped up in it that individual students are neglected! The same basic premises apply to a distance education course—keep the lines of communication open, and always be well prepared.

1.1 Online lingo 101

Is your ISP up and your URL down? Not sure if you need to know the difference between HTTP and HTML?

This section is not meant to be read from Analog-World Wide Web; rather, it is a list of the most common technical terms associated with distance education and the Internet. As a part-time faculty member assigned to teach in an online program, do you need to know all of the terms before you begin your classes? No. You will, however, come across many of these terms while reading this book, and certainly while teaching courses online.

Your Assignment: Skim the list. Stop and read the definitions of a few of the terms with which you may be familiar. Read a few of the terms you've never heard before. Then, refer back to the list, when necessary, while reading.

Extra Credit: Incorporate the necessary terms, where appropriate, into your course description and syllabus. Make sure your students understand and use them correctly.

Analog: A signal that is received in the same form in which it is transmitted, while the amplitude and frequency may vary.

Amplitude: The amount of variety in a signal. Commonly thought of as the height of a wave.

American Standard Code for Information Interexchange (ASCII): A computer language used to convert letters, numbers, and control codes into a digital code understood by most computers.

Asynchronous: Communication in which interaction between parties does not take place simultaneously.

Asynchronous Transmission Mode (ATM): A method of sending data in irregular time intervals using a code such as ASCII. ATM allows most modern computers to communicate with one another easily.

Audio Bridge: A device used in audioconferencing that connects multiple telephone lines.

Audioconferencing: Voice only connection of more than two sites using standard telephone lines.

Backbone: A primary communication path connecting multiple users.

Band: A range of frequencies between defined upper and lower limits.

Bandwidth: Information carrying capacity of a communication channel.

Binary: A computer language developed with only two letters in its alphabet.

Bit: Abbreviation for a single binary digit.

Byte: A single computer word, generally eight bits.

Browser: Software that allows you to find and see information on the Internet.

Central Processing Unit (CPU): The component of a computer in which data processing takes place.

Channel: The smallest subdivision of a circuit, usually with a path in only one direction.

Codec (COder/DECoder): Device used to convert analog signals to digital signals for transmission and reconvert signals upon reception at the remote site while allowing for the signal to be compressed for less expensive transmission.

Compressed Video: When video signals are downsized to allow travel along a smaller carrier.

Compression: Reducing the amount of visual information sent in a signal by only transmitting changes in action.

Computer Assisted Instruction (CAI): Teaching process in which a computer is utilized to enhance the learning environment by assisting students in gaining mastery over a specific skill.

Cyberspace: The nebulous "place" where humans interact over computer networks. Coined by William Gibson in *Neuromancer*.

Desktop Videoconferencing: Videoconferencing on a personal computer.

Dial-Up Teleconference: Using public telephone lines for communications links among various locations.

Digital: An electrical signal that varies in discrete steps in voltage, frequency, amplitude, locations, etc.... Digital signals can be transmitted faster and more accurately than analog signals.

Digital Video Interactive (DVI): A format for recording digital video onto compact disc allowing for compression and full motion video.

Distance Education: The process of providing instruction when students and instructors are separated by physical distance and technology, often in tandem with face-to-face communication, is used to bridge the gap.

Distance Learning: The desired outcome of distance education.

Download: Using the network to transfer files from one computer to another.

Echo Cancellation: The process of eliminating the acoustic echo in a videoconferencing room.

Electronic Mail (E-mail): Sending messages from one computer user to another.

Facsimile (FAX): System used to transmit textual or graphical images over standard telephone lines.

Fiber Optic Cable: Glass fiber that is used for laser transmission of video, audio, and/or data.

File Transfer Protocol (FTP): A protocol that allows you to move files from a distant computer to a local computer using a network like the Internet.

Frequency: The space between waves in a signal. The amount of time between waves passing a stationary point.

Frequently Asked Questions (FAQ): A collection of information on the basics of any given subject, often used on the WWW.

Full Motion Video: Signal which allows transmission of complete action taking place at the origination site.

Fully Interactive Video: (Two way interactive video) Two sites interact with audio and video as if they were co-located.

Home Page: A document with an address (URL) on the World Wide Web maintained by a person or organization which contains pointers to other pieces of information.

Host: A network computer that can receive information from other computers.

Hyper Text Markup Language (HTML): The code used to create a home page and is used to access documents over the WWW.

Hypertext Transfer Protocol (HTTP): The protocol used to signify an Internet site is a WWW site, i.e. HTTP is a WWW address.

Hypertext: A document which has been marked up to allow a user to select words or pictures within the document, click on them, and connect to further information.

Instructional Television Fixed Service (ITFS): Microwave-based, high-frequency television used in educational program delivery.

Integrated Services Digital Network (ISDN): A telecommunications standard allowing communications channels to carry voice, video, and data simultaneously.

Interactive Media: Frequency assignment that allows for a two-way interaction or exchange of information.

Listserv: An e-mail program that allows multiple computer users to connect onto a single system, creating an online discussion.

Local Area Network (LAN): Two or more local computers that are physically connected.

Modem: A piece of equipment to allow computers to interact with each other via telephone lines by converting digital signals to analog for transmission along analog lines.

Mosaic: An example of browser software that allows WWW use.

Multimedia: Any document which uses multiple forms of communication, such as text, audio, and/or video.

Multi-Point Control Unit (MCU): Computerized switching system which allows point-to-multipoint videoconferencing.

Netscape: An example of browser software that allows you to design a home page and to browse links on the WWW.

Network: A series of points connected by communication channels in different locations.

Online: Active and prepared for operation. Also suggests access to a computer network.

Origination Site: The location from which a teleconference originates.

Point of Presence (POP): Point of connection between an interexchange carrier and a local carrier to pass communications into the network.

Point-to-Point: Transmission between two locations.

Point-to-Multipoint: Transmission among multiple locations using a bridge.

PPP: A software package which allows a user to have a direct connection to the Internet over a telephone line.

Protocol: A formal set of standards, rules, or formats for exchanging data that assures uniformity between computers and applications.

Satellite TV: Video and audio signals that are relayed via a communication device that orbits around the earth.

Serial Line Internet Protocol (SLIP): Allows a user to connect to the Internet directly over a high speed modem.

Server: A computer with a special service function on a network, generally receiving and connecting incoming information traffic.

Slow Scan Converter: Transmitter/receiver of still video over narrow band channels. In real time, camera subjects must remain still for highest resolution.

Synchronous: Communication in which interaction among participants is simultaneous.

T-1 (DS-1): High speed digital data channel that is a high volume carrier of voice and/or data. Often used for compressed video teleconferencing. T-1 has 24 voice channels.

T-3 (DS-3): A digital channel which communicates at a significantly faster rate than T-1.

Telecommunication: The science of information transport using wire, radio, optical, or electromagnetic channels to transmit and receive signals for voice or data communications using electrical means.

Teleconferencing: Two way electronic communication among two or more groups in separate locations via audio, video, and/or computer systems.

Transmission Control Protocol (TCP): A protocol which makes sure that packets of data are shipped and received in the intended order.

Transponder: Satellite transmitter and receiver that receives and amplifies a signal prior to re-transmission to an earth station.

Video Teleconferencing: A teleconference including two way video.

Uniform Resource Locator (URL): The address of a homepage on the WWW.

Uplink: The communication link from the transmitting earth station to the satellite.

World Wide Web (WWW): A graphical hypertext-based Internet tool that provides access to homepages created by individuals, businesses, and other organizations.

Figure 1 Faculty checklist

Once you've been hired to teach an online course in your field, and have received the syllabus and textbooks, there is more you need to know. Listed below are some questions you may want to ask the department Chair or Program Director before you begin compiling materials for your online course.

1. What kind of faculty training is offered? Is this training required? Is an electronic competency test required for faculty and/or for students?

2. Which course management software is used?

3. What kinds of automation are available for the instructor?

4. What are the software and hardware requirements for faculty? What are the software (such as Microsoft Word or Access) and hardware requirements for students?

5. Will I be reimbursed for Internet service?

6. What kind of technical support and help are available for adjunct faculty and for students? How soon can I expect a response when I have a problem?

7. What passwords are needed for course and electronic library access?

8. How much of the course content is proscribed?

9. What are my job responsibilities (online training, course design or updating, office hours, live chat, online

departmental meetings, minimum number of days online each week)?

10. How quickly am I expected to respond to student e-mails and postings?

11. What are the limits on class size?

12. Are faculty and students required to post online a certain number of days per week?

13. Is student attendance monitored electronically?

14. Are course textbooks available in electronic format?

15. How do I get copies of the course texts (request from contact person, bookstore, publisher)?

16. Is exam proctoring required?

17. How are grades submitted (online database, e-mail, fax, paper mail)?

18. Who is my contact person? How does this person prefer to be contacted (phone, e-mail, online trouble-shooting form)?

19. Who are some of the other part-time (and full-time) instructors teaching this course online? Are they willing to assist new adjuncts?

20. Who owns my course?

21. Am I eligible to apply for course development sti-

pends? What is the application procedure?

1.2 Technological preparation

Once you've gotten the answers to the questions on your check-list, it's time to evaluate your hardware and software. When it comes to computers, count on Murphy's Law: if something can go wrong, it will. So to avoid crises ranging from delayed access to destroyed data, plan ahead. Having confidence in your tools will increase your own confidence in teaching. Here are a few tips. Share them with your students, as well:

Virus protection: Virus protection software is a necessity, especially if you plan to download any attachments from students onto your home computer. Virus protection is available online for an annual subscription fee (which may be tax deductible); the two leading providers are McAfee (http://www.mcafee.com/us/) and Norton (http://www.symantec.com).

Adware and spyware detection software: Most current computer problems are caused by adware (free software) and spyware (software surreptitiously installed on your computer to track your virtual activity). Among the free tools available to help rid your computer of these electronic parasites are Ad-Aware (http://www.lavasoftusa.com/software/adaware/) and Spybot (http://www.safer-networking.org/en/spybotsd/), which scan your computer and identify intrusive software that is present.

Surge protection: Be sure you have a good surge suppressor that will protect your computer during power surges and lightning strikes. For adequate protection, choose a surge suppressor with a "UL 1449" rating of at least 330V and a joule rating of at least 800V.

Computer back-ups: Be sure to back up all critical information onto CD's or other storage devices such as a USB drive (which is also great for portably storing student papers if you work at different computers). If you don't have a second computer, scout out computers you can use if yours fails: at your workplace, at a friend's or relative's house, at the local college or public library, or at a local Internet cafe.

ISP back-ups: You also need to be prepared for your Internet service to fail. It's good to have a second ISP in place for that eventuality. The best option is to sign up for free limited dial-up Internet service (usually 10 free hours per month) from at least one provider such as NetZero (http://www.netzero.com) or Juno (http://www.juno.com). If you use DSL, your ISP may also offer limited free monthly dial-up service. This webpage offers an extensive database of free ISPs by country: http://www.free-internet.name/index.php

1.3   Design and content preparation

Inexperienced online teachers are surprised by the amount of time involved not only in creating a course, but also in facilitating it. A 1999-2000 study conducted by Belinda Davis Lazarus, a faculty member in education at the University of Michigan-Dearborn, gives some insight into the time commitment required. Lazarus's longitudinal case study found that an experienced instructor of three online education courses spent 3.5 to 7.0 hours per week on each course. The time was spent responding to student e-mails, participating in discussions, and grading.

A significant difference in teaching online is that there is much more advanced preparation necessary. Instructors accustomed to deciding what to do in each class the night before will find the transition particularly overwhelming, for an effective and well-organized online classroom is one where all material is posted from the start. Here are some tips to help ease the transition to the online classroom:

1. Visit sample online classrooms to get a sense of what works and what doesn't, and to better recognize your own online teaching style. Many colleges offer sample course sites for prospective students to explore, but they're also great resources for the adjunct new to online learning. Here are a few, classified according to the course management software used:

WebCT:

◄ St. Mary's University: http://www.stmarys.ca/conted/online/samples.html

◄ Waubonsee Community College: http://www2.waubonsee.edu/public/orientation2/

◀ WebCT exemplary courses: http://www.webct.com/exemplary

Other course management software:

◀ Cerro Coso Community College: http://fall.cerrocoso.edu/ccolsamp/

◀ The Connecticut Distance Learning Consortium sample courses using three course management systems (WebCT, Blackboard, and WebMentor): http://www.ctdlc.org/Sample/guest.html

◀ Northern Virginia Community College: http://www.nvcc.edu/home/lshulman/Rel231/index.htm

◀ University of Mississippi sample course using Angel: http://angel.olemiss.edu/frames.aspx

◀ University of Wisconsin: http://learn.wisconsin.edu/course.asp

◀ University of Wisconsin Stevens Points: http://www.uwsp.edu/natres/nres600/main.htm

◀ Weber State University: http://wsuonline.weber.edu/demo

2. Start simply. You don't have to incorporate all the technological bells and whistles as you begin; trying to do so will only overwhelm you. For example, if you want to incorporate live chat, but aren't sure about how it will work, you can make such interaction an option in your first course rather than a requirement. Once you understand the technology, you'll feel better able to construct a more intricate system of group activities and discussions. The Online Course Design Maturity Model (Neuhauser, 2004) identifies five levels of sophistication and quality across five areas: components and appearance, individualized and personal approach, use of technology, socialization and interactivity, and assessment. The levels of assessment, for example, would progress from no online assignments, to assignments received through e-mail, to test pools, to peer reviews, to more multi-faceted assignments. For more information visit the Summer 2003 issue of *Journal of Interactive and Online Learning* here: http://www.ncolr.org/jiol/issues

3. Set tight and frequent deadlines. Consider segmenting each assignment so that one part of it is due each day. This helps prevent students from procrastinating. Make deadlines absolute, but build in crisis

cushions; for example, you might allow one assignment to be turned in two days late with no penalty, but then penalize students five points for each day other assignments are late no matter what the reason.

1.4 Tips for working efficiently

To save time, set limits on the time spent on the computer; encourage more student-to-student interaction, and make better use of time-saving technology. Here are some specific suggestions:

◀ Block out times during which you will be available to students.

◀ Don't respond to every student on the discussion board. Allow students to moderate discussions; they can answer each other's publicly posted questions so that the instructor isn't always expected to do so. In fact, if you respond too quickly, you can inhibit student responses.

◀ Have students collaborate on group projects. This results in interactions that don't involve the instructor, and in fewer papers to grade.

◀ Save and reuse your discussion board postings from one semester to the next.

◀ Create a FAQ (Frequently Asked Questions) page so that you're not constantly answering the same questions.

◀ Use computer-graded quizzes.

◀ Assemble a body of Internet links related to your course, and build on it each semester through your own searches, as well as by assigning students to compile and annotate a list of course-related Web sites.

◀ Have assignments due at mid-week rather than at the end of the week, especially if you want to stay away from the computer during the weekend.

◀ Make sure students have passed an orientation quiz or completed an online scavenger hunt at the start of the semester so that they know how to navigate the course; this will reduce the number of questions later.

◀ Require that students send work as .txt (text) files if formatting is not an issue, and as .rtf (rich text format) files when formatting is important. This will minimize your download time, and problems related to software conflicts.

◀ Bookmark the course Web site, and write down the password information and tech help phone number; keep both near your computer and in your wallet for when you're working remotely on a computer where this information has not been saved.

Chapter Two

Teaching the Online Student

2.1 Profile of the online learner

According to the National Center for Education Statistics, undergraduates enrolled in distance education courses tend to be older working adults with a demanding and competing set of responsibilities that includes full-time jobs, homemaking, and dependents, in addition to school. Females outnumber males among online students, and the most predominant major is education. These students take online classes for the convenience and because they believe they can squeeze a virtual class into their already bulging schedules. Online students may be enrolled full-time or part-time, and may have all online classes or a mix which includes more traditional classes. They can live across the globe or just down the street from the college. However, students taking all their coursework online are more likely to live in a different state from the institution than students taking only some of their coursework online. While high-speed Internet use has just surpassed dial-up access for the first time (51 percent to 49 percent as of July 2004, according to Nielsen/NetRatings), many students still rely on slower dial-up Internet service providers.

Successful online students need at least minimal computer skills, but colleges typically do not require students to demonstrate technological proficiency before they can enroll in online courses. Visit the home page of any college's distance education program, and you will find some sort of checklist that asks students to screen themselves to check their readiness for online classes. For example, the checklist of J. Sargent Reynolds Community College in Richmond, Virginia, suggests that distance education students possess the skills taught in two computer courses offered by the college. The San Diego Community College District checklist suggests that students should feel comfortable doing the following: word processing, e-mailing, basic file management, downloading software, finding information on the Internet, completing online forms, and using a browser.

Success depends on the extent to which these students are self-directed learners. A frequently cited definition is that "Self-regulated learners are aware when they know a fact or possess a skill and when they do not. Self-regulated students proactively seek out information when needed and take steps to master it. When they encounter obstacles such as poor study conditions, confusing teachers, or abstruse textbooks, they find a way to succeed" (Zimmerman, 1990).

With students who are truly self-directed, you will be a more effective instructor if you create an environment of respected equals, with yourself as more of a guide and facilitator. It is also helpful to offer learning activities that involve such students more actively in the learning process; for example, they prefer the self-discovery of a project to being lectured. Such students respond well to diagnosing their own weaknesses and being guided toward greater competencies in those areas; they appreciate a more individualized program of self-improvement, when possible.

2.2 Handling student conflicts

While self-directed learners tend to make for eager students, they can also have high expectations of the course and the instructor. Add that to the pressure from the competing responsibilities that face returning students, and conflict can arise. Online, such conflict may take the form of nasty e-mails and angry postings. Clashes can erupt as the result of low grades, confusion related to conducting research online, the students' own lack of organizational skills, and team conflicts.

Head off problems from the start: discuss network etiquette, or "netiquette," and offer some rules for appropriate behavior when communicating online. For example, ask them to remember that misunderstanding in electronic communication occurs often. Remind them to be patient and to forgive others' missteps. Encourage

Put Out the Flames

◀ Discuss network etiquette, or "netiquette," and offer some rules for appropriate behavior when communicating online.

◀ Remind students to be patient, and to forgive others' missteps.

◀ Encourage discussion with students about which kinds of behavior are appropriate online.

◀ Ask students to research information about netiquette online, and then to share the best tips they've found.

discussion with students about which kinds of behavior are appropriate online. Ask students to research information about netiquette online, and then to share the best tips they've found.

Even if a student approaches you inappropriately, respond calmly and politely. For example, if you receive a nasty note about the unfairness of a grade, write back and say that you're always willing to discuss issues if approached in a friendly and professional manner, and that you'd be glad to chat if the student would like to send a more appropriate message. This defuses a potentially explosive situation and an apology usually follows; the student has cooled off by that point and is more likely to recognize how the note came across.

If a student "flames," or attacks, another student, step in quickly with a public posting that reminds students about netiquette. Reply privately to the attacker that the postings were inappropriate and to the victim that you are handling the situation.

2.3 Plagiarism and test security

According to the Center for Academic Integrity (CAI), student cheating on college campuses is widespread. In a 1999 survey of 21,000 students on 21 campuses, one-third admitted to cheating on an exam, while half said they'd cheated on a written assignment. Students in the survey also said that cheating is more common in classes where the faculty ignore cheating. Even more troubling for online instructors, 41 percent of the students in a 2001 CAI survey said they had lifted information from online sources without citation.

The Internet has introduced a perplexing problem: while we encourage students in online courses to conduct research, at the same time we fear that the research becomes nothing more than copying— and sometimes a violation of copyright. *Be that as it may, we need to be careful that we do not become overly concerned that students are faking their work.*

Approach the task under the assumption that you have the highest respect and regard for your students. Convey the message to them that you trust them to be honest in completing their assignments, and at the same time build in safeguards. Gary Wheeler (Wheeler, 2002) quotes research which suggests concepts for establishing a creditable learning community. These concepts, which should be communicated to students, are:

1. honesty

2. responsiveness

3. relevance

4. respect

5. openness

6. empowerment

On the other hand, even while assuming the best of our students, we are also responsible for making certain that they do not, for instance, cut and paste from Web sites. To do this, some instructors use proctored exams, during which a monitor supervises the exam to ensure academic honesty. Others make use of Web services that can track down cribbed sources. The Plagiarism Resource Center at the University of Virginia (http://plagiarism.phys.virginia.edu/), for example, offers free software for detecting plagiarism. Some commercial services include TurnItIn (http://www.turnitin.com) and iThenticate (http://www.ithenticate.com), but a more convenient approach is to customize assignments.

Here are some strategies:

◀ Randomized tests: Use courseware that allows you to randomize the order of questions and answers, and to pull questions from a test bank so that each test is different.

◀ Limited test functions: To discourage sharing of tests, use the courseware functions that prohibit printing of test pages, that reveal only one test question at a time, and that do not reveal the test questions on the graded exam.

◀ Timed tests: Timed tests also discourage sharing.

◀ Personal input: Ask questions that require students to illustrate a concept with examples from their own experiences.

◀ New tests: Change tests from semester to semester.

◀ Group tests: Allow collaboration on an untimed test.

◀ Oral tests: Give "chat" tests in which you question each student online about course concepts.

◀ Ungraded self-tests: Increase students' confidence levels—and suppress the feeling that they must cheat to pass—by providing plenty of opportunities for self-testing to let them know if they have mastered the course concepts; for these kinds of tests, use multiple choice, true-false, or matching so that students can easily grade themselves.

◀ Varied test types: Give different sorts of tests, including both timed and untimed, proctored and unproctored, individual and group, as well as formats such as multiple choice, true/false, fill-in-the blank, and essay.

◀ Unusual paper topics: For research papers, provide a list of unusual assignment topics from which students can choose. Encourage original, critical thinking by asking students to try to answer unresolved questions such as "What is the best way to solve our current energy crisis?" or "Why has the U.S. been unable to capture Osama bin Laden?" or "Which South American country would be most suitable to host the Summer Olympics?" Provide a specific case study for analysis, and instead of simply gathering information, students will have to use what they learn to provide their own insights.

◀ Recipe assignments: Require an annotated bibliography or a particular documentation style. You can also create a "recipe" for each assignment. One paper, for example, might require a table, photograph, or illustration; a personally conducted survey or interview; and eight sources, all within the last fifteen years and three within the last five years. In addition, all sources must be attached to the assignment.

◀ Assignments in stages: For students with poor time-management skills who feel pressured to cheat because they run out of time, structure assignments in stages. It's also helpful to set a due date early in the semester, before students are overwhelmed with assignments for other classes.

◀ Post-assignment discussion: Once a paper is turned in, ask students specific questions about their topics and purposes, and how they conducted their research. You can also ask students to write essays about what they learned from completing an assignment. If you prefer a less formal approach, require an online group discussion about an assignment, or request an individual response about the assignment from each student via phone or e-mail. Require multiple short assignments in lieu of one longer paper or test.

◄ Research instruction: Make clear to students how to use information gathered online. Help them make use of the technology without copying it by setting up their own database, which might include the source, subject, keywords, and abstract. You can also help students by leading them to your library's online databases, which are often password-protected and thus a bit harder to reach until students request the passwords from the library. Without such guidance, students will be more likely to conduct general Web searches, and to stumble upon complete essays they may find too tempting to resist.

◄ Familiarity with student writing: Through discussion board postings and other informal assignments (which would not be likely to be plagiarized), you can come to know your students' writing and thinking abilities. As a result, it becomes much easier to recognize work that is not the students' own. If you utilize a written "icebreaker," it may be of value in identifying student writing.

Chapter Three

TECHNOLOGY

The increased use of technology in recent years ranks among the most dramatic changes in education. One needs merely to walk through a modern university building and view the number of computer labs to grasp this fact. The use of technology in higher education has grown so rapidly that there is a concern that there are too many technological options available for incorporation into one's courses. Without proper planning, this may become a problem. Your students, for instance, may rely on different versions of software or Internet search engines.

To be successful, you must view technology as an asset—not a detriment to good communication with students. Keep in mind that it is crucial to provide consistent feedback to all students. Most important, of course, you must be alert very early to identify students who may be having trouble, not due to their capability, but due to their difficulty with the technology.

Here's a list of the tools of distance education that you will need a command of:

3.1   Internet

A quick, reliable online connection is vital to your work as an online instructor. Connecting via DSL (digital subscriber line) or cable is not only much faster than dial-up access, but it also allows you to use the telephone while you're online. This means that when a student calls with a question, you can easily log on to the course for reference. You need unlimited Internet access, which has become the industry standard. Be sure that your ISP (Internet Service Provider) is reliable and offers around-the-clock technical support.

3.2   E-mail

If your course software includes electronic mail, direct your students to use it to contact you; this helps keep all the communication for each course in one spot, and makes for easy referencing later. If the college for which you're teaching gives you a college e-mail address, use that account for all communication with college personnel, and be sure that you know how to access the account remotely. If you do have a college e-mail account, remember to check it daily. You may also want to give students and others an alternate e-mail address for use when the college server is down; this can be your home e-mail address, or you may want to set up a temporary account at a free service such as http://www.hotmail.com. One other reminder about e-mail—sort mail into folders (one for each class or for each student) for easy management. Gary Wheeler, writing in *A Handbook for Adjunct/Part-Time Faculty and Teachers of Adults* (Greive, 2006), gives some good advice for using e-mail with students. It is:

◀ Establish processes and expectations for e-mail use by your students that include guidelines regarding tone of language, frequency, educational purpose, and format.

3.3 Instant messaging

Instant messaging, or IM, refers to text messages sent in real time, a method by which you and a student can instantly contact each other when you are both online. Among the free IM services from which to choose are Yahoo, MSN, and AOL. If you've told students which program you're using (such as MSN), what your screen name is, and when you'll be online, they can send you questions during that time; an instant message will pop up on your computer, and you can answer immediately. You might want to set up your computer to sound whenever you have a message.

3.4 Chat rooms

Chat rooms are good places online for teams to discuss projects in real time; assign group roles and address any confusion that may arise when a group first forms. Deal with conflicts as they arise. Encourage students to interact through a space on your site or in temporary Yahoo chat rooms (which they can set up by going to http://www.yahoo.com). Make sure that students always post a transcript of their chat room sessions on the discussion board so that you can monitor their progress. As an instructor, you can also use the chat room for online office hours; you enter a designated chat room and keep that window open on your desktop so that you can answer questions from any student who also enters at that time.

3.5 Blogs

Short for "web logs," blogs are public journals available online through blog sites or on personal Web sites. Their appeal is that they are constantly updated and provide a way to follow personal stories, as well as to measure social temperatures on current issues. You can use them in your teaching as writing or reading assignments, and you may want to read and even participate in blogs related to teaching online. A free, easy tool to have your students create and post their own blogs is available at http://www.blogger.com. Because a blog is a public record available to anyone with Internet access, blog postings are different from discussion board postings. The larger audience and the more personal nature of blogs make them an option to offer students interested in creating something that will last beyond the end of the term. Two other free blogging sites are http://www.livejournal.com and http://www.easyjournal.com

3.6 Listservs

Automated mailing lists, listservs allow for discussions via e-mail on specialized topics of interest. You can seek advice about problems you are having in the online classroom by joining a distance education listserv. While inactive listservs aren't very helpful, those that dump hundreds of messages a day into your inbox quickly become impossible to manage, so you may want to try out a few services before you settle on the one that best matches your needs. See the section on "Listservs and other discussion forums" near the end of this handbook for some specific listserv resource suggestions.

Chapter Four

COURSE DEVELOPMENT AND PLANNING

When developing and planning your course, much will depend on what you are given to start with. If your course has already been created, and you are bound to use it as is, you may simply need to substitute some of your own personal information. If you're given another instructor's course as a model, you may have more freedom to make changes in both the nature of the course assignments and in the course design. Some established courses use a module format. Some are e-Packs, customizable online course packages created by publishers for online courses. While e-Packs are "customizable," you may or may not be able to adapt them for your use, depending on the complexity of the process for making changes, and whether your college permits alterations in the course material.

If you are given a template, there may be certain design requirements and a general syllabus, but you may be expected to do a lot of the actual course building. However, there's always the chance that you'll be asked to create a class from scratch.

Simplicity and consistency of design is key. What follows is some advice to help with course development and modification. Let's start with a model distance education syllabus (Figure 2).

Figure 2 Model Distance Ed. Syllabus

Course Information
Course title: English Composition II
Course number: ENG 102
Course description: This course presents the development of writing skills through logical organization, effective style, literary analysis, and research. An introduction to the literary genre is also included.
Course date: Thursday, January 13, 2008 through Monday, May 2, 2008
Location: Internet Course
Prerequisite(s): English 101

Instructor Information

Name: Evelyn Beck

E-mail: beck.e@ptc.edu (WebCT e-mail preferred)

Virtual Office Hours: Monday, Tuesday and Thursday 11:00 a.m.-12:00 p.m., Wednesday 7:00-8:00 p.m.

Phone Number: 864-941-8450

Required Instructional Material

Required Textbook: *Literature: An Introduction to Reading and Writing,* Edgar V. Roberts and Henry E. Jacobs (editors), Prentice Hall, 7th edition/2004, 0-13-048584-5

Course-Related Competencies: ENG 102 teaches students to communicate effectively through reading, writing, speaking, and listening; employ effective processes for resolving problems and making decisions; deal effectively and appropriately with others; exhibit professionalism; and demonstrate the ability to function as an independent learner in appropriate situations.

Course Goals: ENG 102 teaches students to use a process approach to produce a polished piece of writing; write an organized literary analysis, using an introduction with thesis, a body, and a conclusion; analyze literature using personal experience, literary terms, and reasoning skills; apply the rules of standard English to writing; recognize characteristics of the different literary genres; locate reference materials to aid in analysis and document sources of information properly.

Course Objectives

UNIT I: WRITING ESSAYS

The students will:

Use a disciplined process when composing by planning, drafting, and revising essays which include introductions, bodies, and conclusions.

Use, in combination with effective content, correct, standard English.

Write essays on setting, character/characterization, point of view, symbol, theme, etc.

Read different types of essays and fictional works critically and examine them for audience, purpose, and techniques.

UNIT II: RESEARCHING WITH DOCUMENTATION
The students will:
Use appropriate documentation.
Use a dictionary and other reference materials to locate information.

UNIT III: DISCUSSION
The students will discuss reading assignments in class.

Course Policies

Introduction and Attendance Policy: Participation is the lifeblood of an online course. You are expected to participate in weekly discussions, to keep up with deadlines for other assignments, and to check e-mail regularly. Students must log into the course at least once a week. Failure to do so may result in the student being dropped from the course. Many financial aid sources require students to submit signed attendance sheets either weekly or monthly. Instructors use course management tracking tools to establish that a student has met the attendance requirement.

College Honor Code

College Online Honor Policy: Include your college's written policy here.

Plagiarism: Plagiarism is submitting all or part of another's work as one's own in an academic exercise such as an examination, a computer program, or written assignment. It is considered plagiarism if you use even a phrase or the same sentence structure as your source, even if you document the source. To avoid plagiarism, you must use your own words and your own sentence structure, and you must credit the source for any ideas that are not your own. Instructors may use Turnitin.com for the detection of plagiarism.

Assessment

Mid-Term Grading Scale: At the mid-point of each term, the instructor will assign a mid-term grade for each student. The following grade designations will be used: S = Satisfactory; M = Marginal; U = Unsatisfactory; W = Withdrawal

Final Grading Scale: At the end of each term, letter grades are given in all courses to indicate the quality of work done by the student. The following grade designation will be used: A = 94-100; B = 85-93; C = 75-84; D = 70-74; F = 69 and below; W = Withdrew; WF = Withdrew Failing

An I (Incomplete) grade may be awarded at the instructor's discretion if only a small portion of your work remains incomplete due to extenuating circumstances. You will be awarded a W (Withdrawal) if you officially withdraw in good standing up through midterm. After midterm, if you quit attending class without notifying the instructor or if your average is below 70, you may earn a WF (Withdrawal Failing).

Technical Support

How to get technical help: To learn more about WebCT, testing your computer and other technical support information visit http://www.ptc.edu/dlGetting_Help.htm

Accommodations

Section on Accommodations for ADA: Students with documented disabilities needing accommodations are encouraged to discuss their needs with the instructor either by e-mail or by making an appointment during office hours and by contacting the designated counselor in the college's Student Success Center at (864) 941-8641 or at http://www.ptc.edu/. Confidentiality of student's disability is maintained in accordance with the Family Educational Rights and Privacy Act of 1976.

Confidentiality of E-mail & Online Materials

All students' e-mail addresses may be available to other students in the class. Although some assignments in an online course may require peer communication, the instructor will make every effort to protect the confidentiality of any personal communication. However, students should recognize that e-mail and other electronic media are never totally secure, nor guarantee of the privacy of your e-mail.The use of Piedmont Technical College's website, e-mail service and WebCT software for the creation and/or distribution of material not pertaining to course participation is prohibited and may be grounds for disciplinary actions according to College Policy. Such actions include, but are not limited to, the inappropriate use of e-mail and discussion boards for harassment, unlawful solicitation, and "spamming" and use of editing tools within WebCT software to create offensive material and/or to link to inappropriate materials.

4.1 Course Development

When you agree to develop an online course (and adjuncts at many colleges are encouraged to submit proposals via the colleges' distance education Web sites), you will receive a course development contract. These contracts all look different. Each college adopts its own contract standard and incorporates the elements it deems most important. However, almost all course development contracts address the following areas:

◀ Payment: The stipend for developing a course may be a set fee (typically ranging from $1,000 to several thousand dollars), or it may be an hourly fee at the usual adjunct rate–with the number of hours already calculated. The payment for developing the course is often the same as what you would be paid for teaching that same course one time. Be sure to check if payment will be given in one or several installments. If payment is to be issued upon completion of the course, be sure it's clear upon whose approval the course is considered complete. In addition, find out if any additional stipend is given the first time you teach the course in order that you might make necessary changes.

◀ Training: The contract may stipulate that you attend specific training to prepare you to develop a course. Whether it does or not, ask about how to get help as you create the course.

◀ Deadlines: Be sure that adequate time is allowed for development. Ideally, you will need at least one quarter or semester to prepare the entire course. Check for preliminary deadlines; be sure you understand what parts of the project are due at each stage. Ask how soon you can expect feedback at each stage, as well.

◀ Description: The contract should outline the required elements of the course you will be developing. This will probably include such items as the syllabus, objectives, study guide, lesson plans, lectures, and exams or other assessments. You may also be required to submit planning materials such as storyboards or scripts, and perhaps descriptions of technology needs. Alternate sets of assignments may also be requested.

◀ Ownership: Pay special attention to what the contract says about who owns the course. In all likelihood, your use of the college's resources to develop the course will entitle the institution to full ownership. However, it is possible that ownership might be shared jointly or that ownership will be yours initially. If you do retain any ownership, ask about how royalties will be shared.

4.2 Storyboards

A storyboard is a plan. It can be as simple as a flow chart, and it can feature only text, though the use of even rough illustrations can provide additional clarity for an instructor to imagine how a course should be presented online. A storyboard is especially useful as a kind of outline before designing a course in order to create clear navigation for students.

The advantages of using a storyboard for planning rather than jumping right into site construction are several. First, storyboarding allows you to clarify goals for each part of your course and then to analyze the style and format in which you want to achieve those goals. Then, storyboarding helps you organize your material into modules and next to identify the online tools that your students will need. Finally, as you create the storyboard, problems will appear more obvious—don't they always on paper? You'll be able to identify and correct those problems more easily. This process can ultimately ease frustration so you don't feel overwhelmed and get lost in your own creation. (The advice of most course designers is to simplify. Limit the elements on any single screen so that scrolling is unnecessary; instead, break the information down into two or three linked screens.)

The simplest way to start is to take the syllabus (yours or the department's) and figure out how you want its elements sorted on your site. For example, some instructors release all material right away, while others make sure that students demonstrate their proficiency before the next unit's material is released to them. Some instructors place all PowerPoint presentations on one organizer page and all case studies on another, while others might group according to topic, placing a PowerPoint presentation and a case study related to Enron on one organizer page, for example. The key is to plan. See Figure 3 for a sample flow chart storyboard format and Figure 4 for a sample outline storyboard format.

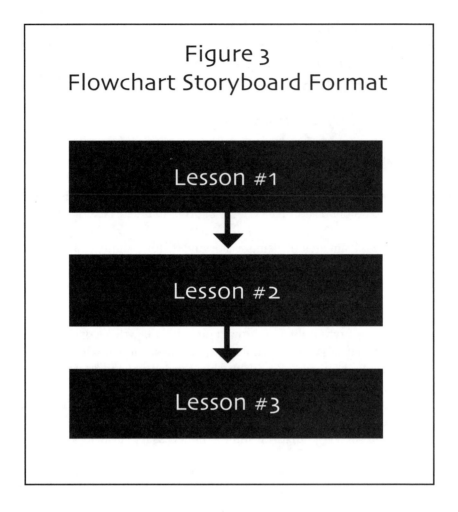

Figure 3
Flowchart Storyboard Format

For more information, here are some links to storyboard templates:

◄ For those who like lists: http://oit.wvu.edu/itrc/coursedev/production/blank_sboard.html

◄ A simple outline with space for a written description and a list of related graphics: http://www.matter.org.uk/storyboard/template.htm

◄ For those who think visually as they plan the layout of each Web page: http://chd.gse.gmu.edu/immersion/lao/fall2000/storyboards/template.html

◄ A detailed worksheet that leads you step by step through plan-

---

Figure 4
Outline Storyboard Format

Lesson # _____

Goals: _____

_____

ON SCREEN: _____

Content:_____

_____

Images: _____

_____

Links: _____

_____

---

ning your online course: http://www.uncc.edu/webcourse/sb/worksheet.htm

Here are links to some sample completed storyboards:

◄ A combination of text and flow chart that helps plan how an individual Web page will be laid out: http://www.usoe.k12.ut.us/curr/ednet/training/materials/syllabus/Lesson8.html

◄ A flow chart in which each box describes one Web page: http://www.uncc.edu/webcourse/sb/storyboard.htm

◄ A graphical flow chart that uses symbols to represent each kind of course activity: http://www.uncc.edu/webcourse/sb/sample2.htm

◄ A hand-drawn storyboard using index cards and rough illustrations: http://www.uncc.edu/webcourse/sb/sample3.htm

4.3 Copyright issues

Copyright laws related to distance education were clarified in 2002 with the passage of the Technology, Education and Copyright Harmonization Act (the TEACH Act), part of the Justice Department Reauthorization Act.

In general, original works, except those in the public domain, such as government works or those whose copyright has expired (usually seventy years after the author's death), are protected by copyright law and cannot be used except in very limited ways.

The provision in the new law to which you should pay special attention is that if you include copyrighted material under the "fair use" standard, you must abide by the following restrictions: If you allow students access to material, their access must be limited to a short time period and they must not be allowed to print or store that material in any way, even as a study tool at a later point. The limits on the time period for an online course are not specifically stated, but the safest course of action is to provide only temporary access to copyrighted material. Check with your distance education administrator about how to limit student access to parts of your site and how to disable print options for some material.

As for what constitutes fair use, that's debatable. If a work was published up through 1922, it's in the public domain and may be used freely. If a work was published between 1923 and 1978, it may or may not still have copyright protection. When a work is still under copyright, you need to evaluate whether your use is "fair" or whether you must seek permission to use the work. A good way to do this is to take the test at http://www.utsystem.edu/ogc/intellectualproperty/copypol2.htm#test, which asks you to decide where, on a scale, your purpose falls related to what kind of work it is; how you will use it; how much of it you will use; and what effect your use will have on the market for the original.

Remember also that you may not scan or upload full or lengthy works, and access to the course must be limited to enrolled students. In addition, you need to post a notice to students that materials used in connection with the course may be subject to copyright protection. (This note might instead be posted by the college on the distance learning main page.)

Even if you violate copyright laws out of ignorance, you are still liable. If found guilty, the fines for each act of "willful infringement" may be as high as $150,000.

An excellent overview from the American Library Association, called "Distance Education and the TEACH Act," is available at http://www.ala.org/ala/washoff/woissues/copyrightb/copyright.cfm. The perspective of attorney Georgia Harper, "Copyright Law in the Electronic Environment," which includes a good explanation of fair use, is available at http://www.utsystem.edu/ogc/intellectualproperty/faculty.htm.

4.4 Free resources

The Web is rich with free resources for college instructors; the challenge is locating the sites. Here are a few sites created explicitly for higher education faculty for use in courses taught both online and offline. Adapt these ideas to fit your own teaching style. While it's not always explicitly stated on these sites, if you do borrow from any source, you should credit the creator.

◄ CAREO (Campus Alberta Repository of Educational Objects) is a Canadian project with 4,047 learning objects such as a chemistry lab, an interactive geometry tutorial and grammar games: http://www.ucalgary.ca/commons/careo/CAREOrepo.htm

◄ College and University Syllabi Published on the Internet offers syllabi in several dozen categories and is maintained by Chicago State University: http://webs.csu.edu/~amakedon/syllabi/resources/resources.html

◄ Connexions, maintained by Rice University in Houston, Texas, offers over 2,000 modules and 59 courses and welcomes contributions: http://cnx.org/

◄ Maricopa Learning Exchange, maintained by Maricopa Community Colleges in Tempe, Arizona, contains 1,114 "packages" of learning objects: http://www.mcli.dist.maricopa.edu/mlx/

◄ MERLOT, which stands for Multimedia Educational Resource for Learning and Online Teaching, offers over 10,000 Web-based learning materials created and constantly expanded by faculty across the country. Faculty members in fourteen disciplines contribute lesson plans, which are then peer reviewed and rated. Reviewers award up to five stars for course material, based on criteria in three categories: quality of content, potential effectiveness as a teaching-learning tool, and ease of use. It is maintained by the California State University Center for Distributed Learning: http://www.merlot.org

◄ MIT OpenCourseWare includes shareable course syllabi, assignments, and other resources for 701 courses at the Massachusetts Institute of Technology: http://ocw.mit.edu/OcwWeb/web/home/home/index.htm

◄ Online Collections of Syllabi links to both general collections and field-specific collections of syllabi and is maintained by the American Academy of Religion in Atlanta, Georgia: http://www.aarweb.org/syllabus/collections.asp

◄ Syllabus Finder contains over 500,000 syllabi from college courses and is maintained by the Center for History and New Media at George Mason University: http://chnm.gmu.edu/tools/syllabi

◄ World Lecture Hall has course materials for 1,550 courses in 83 categories submitted by professors around the world and is maintained by the Center for Instructional Technologies at the University of Texas at Austin: http://web.austin.utexas.edu/wlh/

Chapter Five

STRATEGIES FOR TEACHING

5.1 Learning styles

Attention to the way students learn is just as important in online classes as it is in the traditional classroom. Yet, while you regularly design face-to-face activities that involve visual and audio components, group work, and physical movement, you may still be relying heavily on the written word when delivering courses through the Web.

Learning-styles theory suggests that individuals process information differently and that instructors can help more students succeed by varying the way they present course material. Measurements of learning styles often make distinctions between minds that process abstract data versus concrete data effectively, and between individuals who best learn in sequence, versus those who more easily comprehend information in chunks. Howard Gardner's theory of multiple intelligences identifies eight kinds of learners (See Figure 5), including those who benefit most from personal interaction, those who prefer quiet reflection, and those who need physical activity for optimal learning.

Figure 5: Multiple Intelligences

Howard Gardner proposed in his 1993 book Multiple Intelligences that people learn differently and that each of us is smart in at least one of seven ways:

◀ Linguistic intelligence (language)
◀ Logical-mathematical intelligence (numbers)
◀ Spatial intelligence (pictures)
◀ Bodily-kinesthetic intelligences (body)
◀ Musical intelligence (music)
◀ Interpersonal intelligence (people)
◀ Intrapersonal intelligence (self)
◀ Naturalist intelligence (nature)

John Buerck directs the computer science program at Saint Louis University. He conducted a study in which he compared the learning styles of students enrolled in two sections of the same computer science class (Programming Logic and Design) taught by the same instructor with the same course requirements. One of the classes was taught on campus, while the other was offered online. After completing Kolb's Learning Style Inventory and a short questionnaire, all students were classified as one of four types of learners: Converger, Diverger, Assimilator, Accommodator.

What Buerck found was that students tended to choose a method of course delivery based on their own learning styles. Those who preferred the traditional face-to-face course were mostly Assimilators (comfortable with theory and abstract ideas), while those who preferred the Web-based course were Convergers (skilled at solving problems and identifying practical applications of knowledge). No Internet students were identified as Divergers (good at understanding multiple viewpoints and generating new ideas), and smaller but comparable numbers of students were identified as Accommodators (skilled at carrying out plans and tasks and undertaking new experiences). For part-time faculty, the study presents some crucial information; pay attention to learning styles when incorporating Internet technology into your curriculums. The study also demonstrates that colleges should help guide students toward the kinds of classrooms that best suit the way they learn.

Of course, the reality is that students are generally free to choose online courses without any required screening. However, many learning style inventories are available and can easily be added to a course Web site so that students are at least aware of how they learn best. Further, adjuncts can make online courses more appealing for all kinds of learners by varying the presentation of course material.

The most common mistake made by part-time faculty who are new to online learning is to underestimate the need for interaction and engagement with and among learners. This is manifested by a failure to include interaction, discussion, or feedback into every online assignment.

In addition to encouraging student interaction, you need to pay attention to the multiple ways that students take in information. For example, for each unit you could provide a trio of alternatives: a PowerPoint outline, transcripts of your lectures, and the lectures themselves, streamed using RealPresenter (or Microsoft Media Player).

In contrast, inundating students with print materials can bore and overwhelm them. Richard Felder teaches chemical engineering at

North Carolina State University, and writes regularly about distance education in his field. In a recent article he wrote, he presents a scenario that shows how an online course could engage a learner in multiple ways. In the example, the student reviews a multimedia tutorial that includes photos and diagrams and poses critical thinking questions, watches a video of the course instructor giving a lecture, retrieves information from a database to build an equation, exchanges e-mail with the instructor, and participates in a chat room with the other members of her group to discuss a joint project.

5.2 Accessibility

Since 1998, when Congress amended the Rehabilitation Act, federal agencies have been required under Section 508 of the law to make electronic and information technology accessible to those with disabilities. Coupled with the older and more inclusive Americans with Disabilities Act, there is a greater emphasis on creating online courses that can be used by everyone.

One of the first things the part-time faculty member can do to make her/his course more accessible is to post in different formats. For example, an assignment may be posted as a Web page and also in PDF format. A lecture may be posted in text and in PowerPoint outline form, but once you've been teaching online for awhile, you'll probably want to go further. For instance, you might create HTML tags for illustrations to help the blind or avoid certain colors for those with color blindness. Look at your entire site and its ease of use for those with various disabilities. Here are some free tools that can help:

◀ A list of the requirements for Section 508: http://www.access-board.gov/sec508/guide/1194.22.htm

◀ Web Accessibility Initiative, a good overview: http://www.w3.org/WAI/Resources/

◀ Advice on how to design more usable Web sites: http://trace.wisc.edu/world/web/

◀ Tips for designing accessible Web sites, divided by disability and tool: http://diveintoaccessibility.org/

◀ **Bobby** checks Web sites for conformity to international accessibility guidelines for individuals with disabilities and offers recommendations to fix problems: http://webxact.watchfire.com/

◄ **CynthiaSays!** is a Web content accessibility validation solution, designed to identify errors in design related to Section 508 standards and the Web Content Accessibility Guidelines. This service is a free accessibility validation tester: http://www.cynthiasays.com/

◄ **Accessibility checklist** from Penn State University offers guidelines for designing or modifying Web pages for accessibility: http://tlt.its.psu.edu/suggestions/accessibility/check.html

◄ **WAVE** accessibility tool allows you to submit Web sites for accessibility testing and also to download a Wave tool for instant checking of other pages: http://www.wave.webaim.org/index.jsp

◄ **Accessible Web Publishing Wizard** converts PowerPoint, Excel and Word documents to accessible HTML: http://cita.rehab.uiuc.edu/software/office/

◄ **Adobe** offers information and tools to make PDF files accessible: http://www.adobe.com/enterprise/accessibility/creating. html

◄ **MAGpie** is a tool for captioning and describing multimedia: http://ncam.wgbh.org/webaccess/magpie/

◄ **Microsoft** offers tutorials for using accessibility features in Windows, Word, Outlook, and Internet Explorer: http://www.microsoft.com/enable/training/default.aspx

◄ **STEP508** is a tool for prioritizing Web site accessibility problems: http://www.section508.gov/index. cfm?FuseAction=Content&ID=155

◄ **Vischeck** allows you to see what Web sites look like for those who are color blind: http://www.vischeck.com/vischeck/

5.3 Community building

In teaching a distance education course you are, in a sense, building your own little community. You are not just the facilitator; you are the mayor. Your #1 goal is to keep the citizens from moving out.

Attrition rates for most distance education programs have been higher than for traditional college courses, with dropout rates as high as 80 percent at some colleges, though this trend is changing as programs mature. Many of the reasons—such as students' inexperience with technology, or insufficient student support services—are beyond a part-timer's control. *However, you can have a tremendous impact on student retention simply by the way you communicate.* The form, frequency, promptness, and tone of written and oral interaction with students are very important. The trick is to create a sense of classroom community. If students feel connected, if they believe that you have a personal interest in them, they will be less likely to drop out. Research by Angie Parker, who teaches at Yavapai College, shows that those students with a higher "internal locus of control," or level of self-motivation, were more likely to complete a course. For students taking distance education courses, such an internal control was even more important, because these students must function more independently.

This self-motivation is a learned trait, but it develops more readily through positive reinforcement; if students in online classes feel that they're alone as they struggle with the technology as well as the course material, they are in greater danger of dropping out. In distance education, Parker concludes, "Instructional intervention can be a powerful tool for accelerating motivational change."

The dramatic increase in the number of online courses at colleges and universities—and the problem of hanging on to students unprepared for this new way of learning—are leading to some research efforts aimed at systematically examining both issues. "Quality on the Line: Benchmarks for Success in Internet-Based Distance Education" (2000), a study by the Institute for Higher Education Policy, recommends that contact between faculty and students be "facilitated through a variety of ways, including voice-mail and/or e-mail" and that "Feedback to student assignments and questions is constructive and provided

The Great Communicator

◀ Phone students at the beginning of the course to answer any questions they may have.

◀ Be polite, open and responsive in communications you have with students.

◀ Give frequent and encouraging feedback.

◀ Be understanding and flexible.

◀ Privately congratulate individual students on good grades. Ask what happened when grades are lower than usual.

in a timely manner." Communication, the study concludes, is key. In discussing community online, Gary Wheeler (Wheeler, 2002) quotes a study by Palloff and Pratt that defines the basic steps for establishing a virtual community. The steps are:

◄ Clearly define the purpose of the group

◄ Create a distinctive gathering place for the group

◄ Promote effective leadership within the group

◄ Define norms and a clear code of conduct

◄ Allow for a range of member roles

◄ Allow for and facilitate subgroups

◄ Allow members to resolve their own disputes.

It appears that allowing students to resolve their own conflicts results in improved communication within the group. Since face-to-face interchange is not possible, online discussions in which students present conflicting viewpoints seem to introduce a degree of emotion into the learning process. However, you must be careful to monitor the conflict so that it does not deteriorate into personal issues and discourage dialogue.

One way to do this to set a positive tone from the start. Instructors can do this by being personal, polite, open and responsive in communications you have with individual students, and with the class as a whole. When responding to students' questions and comments on the discussion board and in e-mail, always use their names, and consider signing messages with your first name, which seems friendlier. Make frequent use of terms like "please" and "thanks." All of this takes extra time, but it's worth it.

While it's a good idea to keep most communication on the discussion board so that you don't end up repeatedly answering the same question, e-mail can be a great tool for personal encouragement and for friendly reminders about assignments that are upcoming or overdue. To keep students on task, send weekly e-mails to those who did not post on the discussion board to let them know their contributions were missed. Another way to encourage communication is to make yourself available at times and in a manner that is most helpful for students. This doesn't mean that, as an adjunct, you need to chain yourself to your computer 24/7, but it might mean that you hold an online office hour one evening a week, perhaps the night before an assignment is due. Make it easy for students to contact you instantly, either in a chat room through the courseware or via Instant Messaging.

Here are some practical tips for fostering good communication in online courses:

◄ Call students on the phone. This is a simple and overlooked "low-tech" tool that can be very effective early in the term, especially for students who haven't gotten started yet. It's a way to show you're interested and to answer questions—usually technical—that may have them stymied.

◄ Build a learning community. Have students post written introductions (and photographs if possible) on the discussion board—and post one yourself. Encourage students to interact with discussions about course material, either through a space on your site or in temporary chat rooms. Create an area online for socializing.

◄ Give frequent and encouraging feedback. You might adapt the practices of a biology instructor at Piedmont Technical College in Greenwood, South Carolina, who holds online office hours, responds to e-mail within 24 hours, gives a range of dates for an exam to be completed, and responds to students individually with their grades and where they stand in the course.

◄ Maximize the use of the discussion board to encourage group interaction. Minimize the use of e-mail for communication, and keep communication on the discussion board as much as possible.

◄ Check in daily to answer questions and redirect discussions if they get off track. Students need to sense your presence though you don't want to intrude. Some instructors post on discussion boards a few times during the week while others write a weekly posting which comments directly on what students have had to say during the week. Even if a problem seems to be developing, hold back, for often the group will resolve its own conflicts and be stronger for it. But if discussions veer wildly off track, post a follow-up question to help recapture the focus.

◄ Be encouraging, understanding, and flexible. Congratulate students on a good grade. Ask what happened when a grade was low. Allow them some time flexibility in completing assignments, if possible. Share a little of yourself. Reach out to students who are struggling. A simple note to a student asking, "Is everything OK? I haven't heard from you in a while," can give a student under great pressure the reassurance that someone cares.

◄ Make class fun. Bramucci (2001) offers many ideas for injecting an impish spirit and for giving students reasons to check into the class more often. For example, he suggests a weekly "Guess who?" feature based on unusual facts gathered by the teacher about each student. "Hide" actual test questions on the site in a sort of "Where's Waldo?" activity. Post teasers about interesting information to be covered in an upcoming lesson. Post holiday greetings. Invite students to submit nominations for a joke of the week.

◄ Use an Icebreaker. Maybe more so than with a class taught face-to-face, an icebreaker can be an asset for distance education classes. It commences communication immediately, gives the students a chance to participate and use the technology, and gives the instructor an opportunity to observe student writing styles.

Chapter Six

VIRTUAL CLASSROOM TECHNIQUES

6.1 Text lectures

As a conscientious instructor, you wouldn't think of spending a class period reading to your students in a monotone from lecture notes that summarize a homework reading assignment. You know that lectures need to capture students' interest. Nevertheless, when it comes to online lectures, that same care is sometimes not applied. If you lack the time to craft an illuminating written lecture for each section of your online courses, you may resort to posting dry lecture notes to your Web sites in the hope that these notes will help students understand the material. However, in the process, you cheat your online students of what you routinely deliver to your in-class students: your sense of humor, your memorable anecdotes to highlight factual information, and your passion for the subject.

Here are some tips to improve your online lectures:

1. Start small. Begin with one lecture for one topic in one class. Otherwise, the prospect of writing dozens of lectures could overwhelm you.

2. Keep it short. It's easy for online lectures to ramble, with links to subtopics that sometimes lead to even more sub-subtopics. Making such information available to students is a good idea, but post these links separately, and limit the lecture to about 1000 words. This will help keep students engaged.

3. Make it personal. Online lectures should convey a sense of the instructor's personality. While certain subjects lend themselves to personal reflections more than others, every good teacher ventures at least an opinion, if not a personal story, during a lecture. Here's an excerpt from a lecture about melody and rhythm by Linda Kobler, an adjunct instructor of music in the Virginia Community College System:

> *When my mother was a teenager growing up in Puerto Rico (in the 1920s) she remembers that young boys would stand beneath the window of their girlfriends and serenade them with a guitar*

and a beautiful melody. My mom remembers how she actually helped out a young guy who was having some trouble with his sweetheart, by composing a lovely tune for him to sing. The way she tells it, the melody worked its magic, and he was forever in her debt. It may be a romantic notion, but there is power in a good melody (http://omnidisc.com/MUSIC/Lecture1.html)

In my lecture about how to use the Internet for research, I [Beck] included the following embarrassing admission to highlight the need for checking a source's authenticity:

A few years ago, I made the very stupid mistake of believing something I'd read online just because it was posted at several different sites. It was supposedly the commencement address given by Oracle CEO Larry Ellison at Yale University in which he said that diplomas are for losers. I then referred to this statement in a magazine article I wrote about how important a college degree was in the hiring process. Unfortunately, the editor didn't discover the problem until after publication, and I was mortified.

4. **Write in a conversational style.** Write it the way you would say it. Here's the opening line of a lecture by Thomas O'Connor, who teaches justice studies at North Carolina Wesleyan College in Rocky Mount, about the stop and frisk law: "Frequently, the police will observe somebody who needs to be checked out" (http://faculty.ncwc.edu/toconnor/frisk.htm). Here's the opening line of a section about the fifth-century conflict between the Greeks and Persians, by Norman Raiford, a history professor at Greenville Technical College in Greenville, S.C.: "What was the beef with the Persians?" (http://wellspring.isinj.com/sample/wciv/wciv1/assignment_3_2.htm).

5. **Draw connections to everyday things.** As you know, comparing new ideas to what students already understand fosters learning. Here's another example from Linda Kobler's lecture on melody and rhythm which links musical scales to fabric:

To use an analogy, then, think of scales as a kind of fabric which is used to make an article of clothing. Some fabrics have associations and lend themselves to certain uses. Given a bolt of burlap you probably wouldn't fashion a wedding gown out of it. Neither would you be likely to use silk brocade to make gardening pants! Scales, in the mind of composers, work much the same way, to suggest broadly the type of musical feeling they wish to create. (http://omnidisc.com/MUSIC/Lecture1.html)

Here's an example from my lecture on writing style in which I [Beck] compare styles of prose to fashion:

When my mind wanders in church, I look at the woman who always wears hats or the high school senior with an amazing collection of scarves to see what they're wearing. There's someone else who's always got an intricate hairstyle. And then there's me—I put on whatever doesn't need to be ironed and try to remember to brush my hair. Each of us has an identifiable style—and that extends to writing.

Here's part of a lecture about linear regression by Amar Patel for a statistics course at the University of Illinois at Urbana-Champaign; he's discussing crickets in order to explain how to find relationships between two variables:

Factoid: Crickets make their chirping sounds by rapidly sliding one wing over the other. The faster they move their wings, the higher the chirping sound that is produced. Scientists have noticed that crickets move their wings faster in warm temperatures than in cold temperatures. Therefore, by listening to the pitch of the chirp of crickets, it is possible to tell the temperature of the air. (http://www.mste.uiuc.edu/patel/amar430/keyprob1.html)

Online lectures offer a slightly different challenge than the oratories you deliver in the classroom. But with a little effort, the experience can be just as rich for your students.

6.2 Audio and video lectures

Audio

Presentations you've been using in the classroom can be brought to life online by adding an audio narrative. This format is great for material that is graphical in nature—such as illustrations, charts, and diagrams—and which would benefit from elaboration. Two online courses at the University of Wisconsin-Madison that have effectively incorporated audio online are an online dairy science course, which includes progressively built graphics, and an online pediatrics course, which offers photographs of doctors treating patients, along with flow charts about communication.

Before audio streaming technology became available in 1995,

any student who wanted to view a multimedia presentation would have had to download huge files *before* listening to them. Streamed files play as they are downloaded. This new technology has streamlined a previously cumbersome process; as a result, audio files are now easily accessible to those without high speed Internet connections.

Creating lectures which incorporate streaming audio technology is a bit involved, however, but well worth the added effort. Your first decision involves choosing which software program to use to create your files. RealMedia, QuickTime and Windows Media are all excellent. You must then find out whether most of the students are using PC's or Macintosh computers. Finally, you must also take into consideration your own technical skills. For tutorials on using streaming media, see http://streaming.wisconsin.edu/understand/understand.html and http://ion.uillinois.edu/resources/tutorials/software/streamingmedia/index.asp.

Most experts recommend that you limit each lecture to about 10 minutes, since online learning often happens in small chunks of time. This allows students to stop, start and replay parts of the lecture as necessary. For variety, you can bring in guest speakers, as the instructor of a Middle English literature class did by recording a scholar reading the opening of *Sir Gawain and the Green Knight*. I incorporated music to add atmosphere in an audio lecture I prepared for my online World Literature students; I included a clip from a Ravi Shankar CD of Indian chants as a prelude to a discussion of the novel *Clear Light of Day*, which is set in India. (Copyright concerns can be minimized if you operate under fair-use guidelines, and if your course environment is password protected.)

Video

Many boring video lectures are available online; before making your own video lecture, conduct a Web search to see for yourself how boring some video lectures can be. You will quickly note that many of the worst offenders have simply filmed themselves giving a lecture; the "talking head" approach is deadly dull. Instead, consider other approaches. For example, record a conversation between you and a colleague on a topic. Organize and film a short panel discussion. Interview experts. Give a demonstration. If you can recruit some fellow actors, dramatize a topic. Have some fun by including costumes in your mini-play. (Consider getting students in a face-to-face section of the class to help as part of a group project or for extra credit.) Include visual props; humor is also a great tool, if used appropriately, and keep the videos brief, no more than 10 minutes long.

For easier access by students who use dial-up Internet service, have the video streamed through your campus's server by contacting a technician in the distance education office.

6.3 Discussions

No matter what the subject area, discussions create a sense of community in online courses. The trick is to create discussion questions that encourage critical thinking, and then to follow up students' responses with questions that encourage them to think ever more deeply about the topic. One way to do this is to pose your questions according to Bloom's Taxonomy, which ranks thinking in six increasingly sophisticated levels (see Figure 6). In terms of discussion topics, you want springboards that are complex, perhaps controversial, and relevant in terms of the content and the students' interests and experiences.

Here are some examples of potentially rich types of discussion topics:

◀ Web site evaluation: Ask students to post a link to a good or bad Web site on a particular topic, and explain what is good or bad about the site. Then other students can reply with their perspectives on the linked sites. For example, after discussing sexist language, ask students to evaluate whether a site they've selected contains gender-neutral language. Another example would be a class on Web site architecture that asks students to identify sites that are either easy or difficult to navigate.

◀ Current events: Connect an issue of widespread interest to course material. For example, the post-September 11 debate about whether to restrict immigration would offer a good starting point for discussion about the immigrant narratives students were reading in American literature.

◀ Controversy: Make a current controversy the topic of a debate. A biology class might debate whether stem cell research should be allowed; a criminal justice class might tackle the use of stun guns by police officers.

◀ Role play: Give a hypothetical situation, and ask different students to assume roles in the discussion. An education class might

Figure 6: Bloom's Taxonomy

Use Bloom's Taxonomy to create more difficult questions as the term progresses:

Knowledge (ask questions that begin with words like list, define, tell, describe, identify, show, label, examine, tabulate, quote, name)

Comprehension (ask questions that begin with words like summarize, describe, interpret, contrast, predict, associate, distinguish, estimate, differentiate, discuss, extend)

Application (ask questions that begin with words like apply, demonstrate, calculate, complete, illustrate, show, solve, examine, relate)

Analysis (ask questions that begin with words like analyze, separate, order, explain, connect, classify, arrange, divide, compare, select, explain, infer)

Synthesis (ask questions that begin with words like combine, integrate, modify, rearrange, substitute, plan, create, design, invent, compose, formulate, prepare, generalize, rewrite)

Evaluation (ask questions that begin with words like assess, decide, rank, grade, test, measure, recommend, convince, select, judge, explain, discriminate, support, conclude, compare, summarize)

assume roles of parents, students, administrators, and school board members engaged in a discussion of the merits of instituting a new dress code policy or a year-round school calendar.

◀ What if?: Offer students a fantasy question that encourages a creative approach to the material. For example, ask literature students to imagine how three specific characters would react if thrown together in a lifeboat, or what might happen after the end of another story.

◀ Statistical analysis: Give some interesting facts and ask students to analyze them. For example, using the *Statistical Abstract of the United States*, a world history class might look at world population figures, and discuss the reasons why African population growth continues to outpace the rest of the world.

◄ Exemplification: Ask students to provide examples from the reading or from their own experience to illustrate a concept. For example, teach grammar by calling on students to write sentences illustrating particular rules.

◄ Case study: Post a case study and ask for analysis. In a business communications class, students might receive a scenario about an employer having problems with excessive employee absences during the summer, which was his busy season. They would discuss possible solutions to the problem.

Once students have posted their replies to the topic, it's important to follow up with questions that push them further. Muilenburg and Berge (2002), citing earlier research by L.B. Savage, offer these examples of probing follow-ups:

◄ What reasons do you have for saying that?

◄ Why do you agree (or disagree) on that point?

◄ How are you defining the term that you just used?

◄ What do you mean by that expression?

◄ Is what you are saying here consistent with what you said earlier?

◄ Could you clarify that remark?

◄ When you say that, what is implied by your remarks?

◄ What could follow from what you just said?

◄ Is it possible you and he are contradicting each other?

◄ Are you sure you're not contradicting yourself?

◄ What alternatives are there to such a formulation?

A course with many students and with active discussions can quickly become time consuming. To keep the workload manageable, remember that while it's important for the instructor to participate, you don't have to—and shouldn't—respond to every posting or to every student. In fact, doing so prevents students from taking ownership of the information; they reply less often to each other, and rarely look to one another for insight. Discussions become much less vital and less democratic, and undercut the universal participation that is one of the great advantages of online classes. You can get students even more involved—and save yourself some work—if you make them individually, or in groups, responsible for some of the discussion topics; they can post the topic, respond occasionally to foster further discussion, and post a summary once the discussion is over.

To keep the discussion board organized, create distinct threads for different topics. Use a separate thread for questions and announcements. You may also want to create a thread just for personal exchanges, a kind of student lounge where they might share accomplishments and commiserate over disappointments. Another option is to create an anonymous thread, where students can feel uninhibited about posting concerns about the course.

To ensure participation, discussion postings must be required. Make clear how often students must post, and give them specific guidelines about the quantity and quality (along with a model) of an acceptable response to the topic. You can also model such responses through your own postings.

To ensure interaction, you may want to require that students reply to a minimum number of classmates per topic or per week. Students especially need guidelines on these replies so that the discussion doesn't consist of postings like "good comment." They need help in understanding how to add specific information that expands and deepens the discussion. Encourage them to respectfully disagree with one another, since debates make for the most interesting discussion, and encourage them to offer personal anecdotes that illustrate the discussion topic; for example, in a class in which students read some nonfiction about racism, several students wrote about experiences in which they felt they had been mistreated because of their race.

To help students become proficient at this kind of interaction, post a model interaction, and model such replies yourself. Reply to some of the student comments applauding specifically what was so good, and for the first few weekly summaries, include examples of excellent replies. To get students to read carefully, and to value their classmates' postings, you might require that in one of their papers, students must refer specifically to (and document) a classmate's posting relevant to their topic.

A few more tips:

◀ **Deadlines:** Set rigid deadlines. Use weekly topics, with no credit for postings once the week ends, no matter what the reason. (To allow for unavoidable crises that will arise, however, late in the semester you might offer everyone an extra credit assignment equal in value to the grade for one week's postings.)

◀ **Informality:** Make clear that while an error-free posting is easier to read, students need not worry excessively about grammar, spelling and punctuation for discussion board postings. The discussion board is a place to explore ideas more informally while other assignments require higher standards of perfection.

◀ **Summary:** Post a summary at the end of a discussion topic to provide closure and to reinforce what was learned. Praise (by name) some of the most insightful postings.

◀ **Ascending complexity:** Structure discussion questions to make them more challenging as the term progresses.

6.4 Chat

While most aspects of online classes are asynchronous, with students working independently at times convenient for them, some researchers support the use of live chat sessions. Wang and Newlin (2001) tout chats as an ideal two-way communication that facilitates real instruction that "takes the 'distance' out of distance education." Chats allow for an interpersonal closeness, immediacy and excitement that can't be achieved through asynchronous discussion. Chats offer the chance to give immediate feedback and encouragement, and to correct misconceptions; they also provide an opportunity for student-to-student small talk that might not occur otherwise. This kind of forum helps students feel more connected to their classmates.

You can use chats as review sessions and to explore new topics. English instructors have also used them as mini-writing workshops. Classmates help each other narrow essay topics, or help one another understand the opposite perspectives in a persuasive essay on a controversial current issue.

The problem with live chats is scheduling them. Some institutions, such as Kaplan College, have made weekly hour-long chats a course requirement. Students sign up for a class that has a chat session that fits their schedule. If you teach at an institution which doesn't have a chat requirement, though, it may be a challenge to find a chat time that suits everyone. To get around that obstacle, you can schedule multiple chats on the same topic. This allows students to find the time that works best for them. Another alternative is to schedule several chats on different topics and at different times throughout the term and to require that students attend a certain number (perhaps half) of them. Conversely, you can make the chats optional, though attendance likely will not be high in that case. Another option is to hold several chats at different times during the semester. Require attendance at all, but offer students unable to participate the option of summarizing the session from a transcript.

Chat tips:

◀ An ideal online chat session will last 60 minutes—long enough to cover one or more topics in some depth.

◀ Note the days and times when your students tend to be online, and schedule a chat at that time.

◀ Before the chat session begins, open documents that you want to post during the chat, and keep them minimized on your desktop for quick access. Since these sessions move so quickly, you'll want something you can quickly copy and paste into the chat room.

◀ Post chat transcripts so those who can't attend will benefit.

6.5 Guest experts

Even online, the voice of a single course instructor can grow wearisome over the length of a semester. One way to hold student interest, and invigorate your own teaching, is to invite guest experts to interact with your class via discussion boards or chat rooms. The Internet makes it easier for guest experts to participate from any location. Ask guests to respond online to student comments over several days at their convenience. Guests may find such a request easier to grant than delivering a presentation during your on-campus class meeting. However, the process of arranging for guests and helping them to prepare can be involved.

Whom should you invite? An instructor of an agribusiness management course with an Internet component at the University of Idaho, in Moscow, uses his industry contacts to find agribusiness managers, lenders or consultants. Each guest expert e-mails in a discussion question, which the instructor then posts online. Then the students engage in an asynchronous, threaded discussion, first with the expert, then among themselves. An education professor at the University of Maryland, in Baltimore, invites the author of the book or chapter currently under study. He uses audio or computer conferencing, sometimes in real time but more often asynchronously, with students asking questions for the guest's reaction. At the Air Command and Staff College, a professional military education program for mid-career officers located at Maxwell Air Force Base in Alabama, guests deliver a live lecture for resident students; for nonresidents, the lecture is videotaped, digitized and put on a course CD. Guests have ranged from General Anthony Zinni, who briefed the students on the United States Central Command, to Andy Rooney, who discussed his military experiences and the media's relations with the military.

Guest experts need not be prominent in their professions. One obvious source is other faculty on your campus. Your college communications department might even have a list of faculty who have agreed to serve as guest speakers when asked. Manufacturers, trade associations, and publishers would probably be delighted for the promotional opportunity. Consider community leaders or agency representatives. However, be sure that whoever you ask has Internet access.

The best topics are open-ended ones which might involve controversy. Discussion topics should, at the very least, ask the question "why" rather than the question "what."

6.6 Real-time data assignments

Real-time data—widely available online for subjects ranging from earthquake and hurricane activity to computer industry returns—offer you a dynamic source of information which changes frequently, sometimes hourly.

In economics classes at North Carolina State University in Greensboro, N.C., students try to predict who will win an election, whether the Federal Reserve is going to raise interest rates at its next meeting, or what the box office receipts of a movie are going to be in its first four weeks of release. Using real-time data Web sites such as the Iowa Electronics Market, students make weekly virtual trades, then report on their reasoning as well as the outcomes of their decisions. With movies, for example, students try to develop a statistical model to predict box office returns. Based on such factors as the appeal of pre-release trailers and the star power of the leading actors, as well as the overall economy, they decide which film contracts would be the best buys.

The availability of real-time data makes course material much more immediate to the students. A biology class at Paradise Valley Community College in Phoenix, Arizona, uses data related to El Nino, hurricanes, temperatures, ozone, ocean currents, and state streams and rivers. At Georgia Perimeter College in Clarkston, Georgia, a geology instructor sends students online to check worldwide volcano activity. Students select a volcano to track, often picking based on some personal connection, such as travel experience, or relatives living near the site. Then they answer questions about the character of the eruption, the type of volcano and lava, the kinds of rocks forming from it, and how the volcano affects people living in the area. Students supplement their research with news reports, official government warnings, and information from volcano observatories and volcano-monitoring agencies, such as the U.S. Geological Survey.

Given that the vast amount of information you can find online is overwhelming, you might use this as an optional assignment. Be sure to have a back-up site in case the real-time data suddenly become static (such as temperatures that might not produce very dramatic highs and lows when the weather has turned cloudy).

Here are some real-time data Web sites to get you started:

◀ El Nino information: http://www.elnino.noaa.gov/

◀ Iowa Electronic Markets: http://www.biz.uiowa.edu/iem

◀ National Climatic Data Center: http://www.ncdc.noaa.gov/oa/ncdc.html

◀ National Earthquake Information Center: http://earthquake.usgs.gov/regional/neic/

◀ National Hurricane Center: http://www.nhc.noaa.gov/

◀ Ozone data: http://airnow.gov/

◀ U.S. earthquakes: http://earthquake.usgs.gov/recenteqs/

◀ U.S. Geological Survey, National Water Information System:

http://waterdata.usgs.gov/nwis/

◀ Volcano World: http://volcano.und.nodak.edu/

◀ Volcanoes: http://volcanoes.usgs.gov/

◀ World seismicity: http://earthquake.usgs.gov/eqcenter/recenteqsww/index.php?old=world.html

6.7 Virtual field trips

The best educational Web sites, which involve students in a way that helps them become producers of knowledge, make for great virtual field trips.

Here are some destinations where you might send your students:

◀ Geology field trips at http://www.uh.edu/~jbutler/anon/gp-virtual.html take visitors everywhere from the Stone Forest in China's Yunnan Province to the Pleistocene period on Edisto Beach, S.C. You can find out how to screen for fossils, learn such Icelandic words as *foss* (waterfall), and take a fly-by over three-dimensional Alaskan glaciers.

◀ The Tempe, Arizona, Police Department Crime Unit at http://www.tempe.gov/cau/ offers information about crime analysis, as well as crime statistics and trends. Michael Turturice, who teaches a criminal justice class at Tempe's McClintock High School, sends students to this site for information about crime in their own neighborhoods. (More innovative ideas from Blackwell's can be found at http://www.vickiblackwell.com/vft.html)

◀ Multiple historic points of view related to the Civil War's Battle of Antietam can be contrasted at http://www.nps.gov/anti/contents.htm. These include visuals (photographs of the battlefield and monuments), eyewitness accounts, timelines, and military analysis. High school social studies teacher Kelly Fortner uses this and related sites to push students toward narrative and analytical projects. (See more of her ideas at http://www.lessonplanspage.com/SSCICivilWarVirtualFieldTripPlusHyperStudioPres59.htm)

◄ An online tour of The Holocaust Museum at http://www.ushmm.org/ allows visitors to move and examine artifacts, much as an on-site visitor might do. For example, if you choose to follow the links related to Suse Grunbaum, you'll see a photo of the cookbook she kept as a safer alternative to a diary and a photo of her in front of the hiding place under the floorboards of a barn where she and her family stayed for two years.

◄ The Mount Vernon tour at http://www.mountvernon.org/virtual/index.cfm/ss/29/ takes visitors through George Washington's mansion in a systematic manner—from floor plans to individual rooms to individual objects in each room. Accompanying each object is an explanation, often a quotation from Washington himself. This tour could work for an exercise in place description in a composition class or as a complement to classes in architecture or American history.

◄ The National Women's History Museum at http://www.nmwh.org/exhibits/intro.html is helpful for visual reinforcement when American literature students read the *Declaration of Sentiments*. They can examine gold suffrage ribbons and suffrage playing cards (featuring a blindfolded American goddess of justice), and they can also test their knowledge about the early women's movement with a short quiz that asks such questions as "Why were some suffragists jailed?" Answer: for picketing the White House.

◄ Sites with frequently updated data are among the most fun. For example, an astronomy instructor might like to have students check their inspection of the night sky by visiting the Worchester, Massachusetts EcoTarium's virtual planetarium at http://www.ecotarium.org/activities/planetarium/, which charts each night's visible stars and planets.

◄ The Exploratorium at http://www.exploratorium.edu/ is a treat of a different sort. You can learn about step dancing by moving different steps into a sequence of your choice and then viewing the resulting video. You can see how the hunting bow transformed—re-enacted before your eyes—into a Brazilian musical instrument called the berimbau. And you can learn how to forecast surfing conditions at the beach.

◄ The Rock and Roll Hall of Fame Museum is a great resource for lesson plans that use music. At http://www.rockhall.com/programs/plans.asp are ideas for using rock to teach economics, history, critical thinking, literary analysis, composition—and even music.

◄ For a good starting point, check out http://vlmp.museophile.com/, with links to hundreds of online museums from around the globe.

6.8 Problem-based learning/case studies

Case studies and problem-based learning (PBL) have long been regular features of courses in law, medicine, and business. Now they are also gaining popularity as teaching tools for humanizing science, and for helping students think critically as they work their way through the scientific method in solving a problem. In addition, case studies are a great way for science faculty who teach online to encourage critical thinking and to incorporate discussions, writing assignments, and group projects—excellent complements to fact-based Web presentation of material.

PBL offers real-world cases to students, who can work individually or in teams, to unravel the problems. Clyde Herreid, a biology professor and director of The National Center for Case Study Teaching in Science at SUNY Buffalo, has identified three kinds of case studies: dilemmas (such as deciding whether an AIDS drug with serious side effects should be made available to the public), appraisals (such as analyzing the effects of the Exxon Valdez oil spill), and histories (such as examining the Tuskegee syphilis study, a secret government project in which hundreds of African-Americans with syphilis were studied but not treated).

One excellent source of scientific case studies is available at SUNY Buffalo's Web site: http://ublib.buffalo.edu/libraries/projects/cases/ubcase.htm. There, you can find scenarios from many areas of science that can be used for class discussion, debate, team projects, or research studies.

Here are a few examples, along with the name of the educator who wrote each one:

◀ Anatomy & Physiology: Use forensics to identify the sex, age, and height of a skeleton. (*Alease Bruce*, University of Massachusetts at Lowell)

◀ Chemistry: How safe are polycarbonate baby bottles? (*Michael A. Jeannot*, St. Cloud State University)

◀ Ecology: Who should manage the St. Croix River? (*Pamela Locke Davis*, University of Minnesota)

◀ Geology: What are the ethics involved in publicizing scientific discoveries too quickly, such as NASA's 1996 announcement that life existed on Mars? (*Bruce C. Allen and Clyde F. Herreid*, University at Buffalo)

◀ Physics: Use Newtonian mechanics to figure out how a cheerleader can lift up a 300-pound football player. (*Malati Patil*, University at Buffalo, State University of New York).

When using the case-study method, be sure that each case uses dialogue to tell a good story and that it's relevant, contentious, recent, and short.

6.9 Online labs

In virtual science labs, students can handle dangerous poisons, analyze raging rivers, and conduct experiments in evolution—activities otherwise impossible for most college students.

In a virtual earthquake lab at California State University at Los Angeles, students generate a set of seismograms for an earthquake and locate its epicenter by estimating the time interval between the arrival of the P and S waves. In the online science lab for physical geography at Casper College in Casper, Wyoming, students study satellite images and data involving climate, volcanoes, and earthquakes.

Unfortunately, most science instructors agree that wet labs offer an experience that can't be replaced, that sometimes equipment needs to be handled and objects need to be physically manipulated. For many programs, the ideal compromise is a combination of virtual and hands-on lab experiences. At Rio Salado Community College in

Tempe, Arizona, online biology students receive lab kits in the mail. One of the more unusual online science labs is a virtual crime lab that supplements an on-campus course called Chemistry and Crime: From Sherlock Holmes to Modern Forensic Science, at Williams College in Williamstown, Massachussetts. The virtual lab is intended to introduce students to the nature of crime labs before they attend hands-on labs. It is also a way to add order to the chaos that resulted when fifteen lab students coming from different crime scenes engaged simultaneously in six or seven different experiments.

6.10 Games

Using simple games in an online course can offer variety and appeals to the natural pleasure most of us feel when playing a game. In short, games offer a different and particularly effective way to involve students. Games can be used as a kind of self-test for review. Prensky (2001) advises that educational games need rules, goals and objectives, outcomes and feedback, conflict/competition/challenge/ opposition, interaction, and representation or story. Some of the most popular kinds of simple games are crosswords and matching, as well as games modeled after popular TV shows like *Who Wants to Be a Millionaire?*

A number of sites offer free versions of their game software that you can incorporate into your site:

◀ Hot Potatoes, free for educators, allows you to create six kinds of games, including crosswords and matching: http://web.uvic.ca/hrd/hotpot/

◀ Crossword Compiler: http://www.crossword-compiler.com

◀ QuizMaster: 9 games, including Sink the Fleet and TicTac-Toe: http://cybertrain.info/quizman/qmselect.html

◀ Flash Learning Games: http://itc.umcrookston.edu/Flash-Games/Flash.htm

◀ Matching Puzzle: 5 free games including crossword, hangman, slider puzzle, word search and memory squares: http://janmulder.com/

◀ Links to various quiz makers, including PowerPoint templates for creating Jeopardy, The Weakest Link, Hollywood

Squares, and Who Wants to Be a Millionaire?:
http://eleaston.com/quizzes.html#cr

◀ GameMaker, which includes a free version, allows you to design more complex games: http://www.yoyogames.com/make

◀ Eclipse Crossword: http://www.eclipsecrossword.com/

◀ WebAuthor, a tool to create exercises for foreign language instruction: http://ccat.sas.upenn.edu/plc/larrc/webauthor.html

◀ Quiz Center, which hosts your games on its Web site: http://school.discoveryeducation.com/quizcenter/quizcenter.html

◀ Form Builder, free for educators, which allows you to create simple quizzes: http://www.unc.edu/cit/formbuilder/index.html

◀ CASTLE toolkit for creating interactive quizzes:
http://www.le.ac.uk/castle/

◀ Zoomerang, to create surveys: http://info.zoomerang.com/

6.11 Cooperative assignments

Cooperative assignments for distance learning courses should be formatted in much the same manner as those given to students in face-to-face courses. You should structure the groups with several things in mind: all students must participate, you must develop a method to capture individual student participation, and a written product must be the result. As the facilitator, you must contribute through thorough planning and total commitment.

If they're handled well, online projects can mirror real kinds of online collaboration that today's students will face in their careers.

One example of successful online collaboration among students is an online MBA course at Morehead State University in Morehead, Kentucky. Students choose an article from *Fast Company* magazine, post related discussion questions, and then summarize their class-mates' responses. They get together in a live chat area provided by the courseware, and also correspond via e-mail. Another group project they complete is an online press conference, in which half the group represents the media and the other half poses as a company's business managers. For about an hour in the group chat area, they engage in a question and answer session. These students also write case studies of business-related problems using both e-mail and an online drop box where students can exchange documents.

Group activities such as those outlined above work well thanks to "virtual team-building" exercises conducted early in the semester. In these exercises, students discuss group roles, and each student is urged to take on a task, such as taking notes at group meetings or e-mailing meeting reminders to each member. At the end of each group activity, feedback is elicited on the value of the project.

At West Virginia Community College in Wheeling, West Virginia, students in a Web-based biology class work together on a writing project which covers issues such as gene therapy or water pollution. The groups give live presentations at the end of the semester, sometimes with sound clips and animated graphics. A technologically simpler fulfillment of such an assignment would be to have students create PowerPoint slides and to use the speaker's notes function for commentary.

The peer review is another example of group work. Students post essay drafts for evaluation by classmates, according to guidelines set forth by the instructor. Yet another example is the creation of a team Web site on a particular topic, such as one of the authors studied in a literature class.

In group work, students learn to share their talents. According to Bonk, Wisher, and Lee (2003), "The role of the instructor in such an environment is to facilitate students to generate and share information, not to control the delivery and pace of it. A key goal of team-based learning activities, therefore, is to apply expertise and experience of the participants to a group problem-solving situation or research project that helps participants accomplish something that they could not achieve individually."

Another article co-written by Bonk, who teaches instructional systems technology and educational psychology at Indiana University in Bloomington, cites an example of an online graduate education course. Groups had to write an Internet policy for a school district superintendent beset by demands for information access and privacy protection from parents and students.

Group projects increase interaction among students, but place demands upon students' out of class time.

Here are a few tips for facilitating effective groupwork:

◄ Roles: Require each team member to take on a role.

◄ Charter: Get the group to create a team charter, which spells out the expectations of group members, as well as guidelines for how they will communicate and how they'll handle conflict.

◄ Transparency: Insist that all communication be posted on a group discussion board. If the team uses a chat room for live discussion, have them post a transcript on the discussion board.

◄ Feedback: Allow each group member to evaluate his or her teammates at the conclusion of the project. You may or may not include that as a part of the individual's grade.

Chapter Seven

ASSESSMENT

7.1 Exam options

When giving exams, decide if proctors will be required, and if the tests will be timed. Assume that reference material will be used unless you require proctoring. Use variable options in your online exams to appeal to different learning styles. Keep in mind that online automated grading is available only for objective exams. Here are some options:

◄ Ungraded quizzes and surveys for student self-assessment

◄ Multiple choice

◄ Matching

◄ True false

◄ Sequencing

◄ Fill in the blank

◄ Short answer

◄ Essay

◄ Portfolios

◄ Projects

◄ Papers and reports

◄ Group assignments

◄ Presentations

◄ Journal

◄ Problem solving

To help students prepare, post sample exams and sample responses, perhaps from previous student exams if you have secured permission from the students for such use. Provide both superior and inferior student responses, along with commentary explaining the strengths and weaknesses.

7.2 Classroom Assessment Techniques

Classroom Assessment Techniques (CATs) help gauge how well students are learning the material. Informal and ungraded, they solicit specific information about what students do and don't know. While CAT's are a bit harder to administer to online students, getting this sort of feedback in a distance education class is even more valuable. Here are some questions to consider:

◄ **Background knowledge probe**: At the beginning of the term, give students a list of terms related to the course, and ask them to rate their level of familiarity with each one.

◄ **Muddiest point**: At the end of a lesson, ask students to name something they still don't understand.

◄ **Classroom opinion polls**: Ask students what they like and don't like about the class so far.

For more information, consult these sites:

◄ An overview of CATs: http://honolulu.hawaii.edu/intranet/committees/FacDevCom/guidebk/teachtip/assess-1.htm

◄ Descriptions of 8 CAT's: http://www.ntlf.com/html/lib/bib/assess.htm

◄ Over a dozen CAT's: http://www.siue.edu/~deder/assess/catmain.html

◄ 20 CAT's: http://teaching.iub.edu/wrapper_big.php?section_id=assess

Notes

Figure 7
FACULTY SELF-EVALUATION
Semester 1

Grade yourself from A to F on how well you perform in each of these areas in your online teaching.

TECHNOLOGY

I have all the necessary equipment to teach online. _____

I have all the necessary back-ups in place. _____

NAVIGATION

My course is easy to navigate. _____

I have posted information in multiple places. _____

ORGANIZATION

I have posted all information for my course before the

term begins. _____

I check into the course daily or almost daily. _____

COMMUNICATION

I respond to students in a timely fashion. _____

My interaction with students is always personal

and professional. _____

I have been able to create a caring community in my course. _____

PEDAGOGY

I use a variety of activities to appeal to different learning

styles. _____

ASSESSMENT

Assessment is varied and appropriate. _____

I give thoughtful feedback in a timely manner._____

ACCESSIBILITY

I have checked my Web site for accessibility and made

recommended changes. _____

Figure 8
FACULTY SELF-EVALUATION
Semester 2

Grade yourself from A to F on how well you perform in each of these areas in your online teaching. Compare your grades.

TECHNOLOGY

I have all the necessary equipment to teach online. _____

I have all the necessary back-ups in place. _____

NAVIGATION

My course is easy to navigate. _____

I have posted information in multiple places. _____

ORGANIZATION

I have posted all information for my course before the term begins. _____

I check into the course daily or almost daily. _____

COMMUNICATION

I respond to students in a timely fashion. _____

My interaction with students is always personal and professional. _____

I have been able to create a caring community in my course. _____

PEDAGOGY

I use a variety of activities to appeal to different learning styles. _____

ASSESSMENT

Assessment is varied and appropriate. _____

I give thoughtful feedback in a timely manner._____

ACCESSIBILITY

I have checked my Web site for accessibility and made recommended changes. _____

RESOURCES

Journals/Web sites

Stay current in the field by regularly reading the latest research and opinion pieces from experts. Here are some of the best journals and Web sites available:

American Center for the Study of Distance Education, maintained by Penn State's College of Education: http://www.ed.psu.edu/acsde/

American Distance Education Consortium, with a helpful link to "Learning Resources": http://www.adec.edu/

American Journal of Distance Education, abstracts of scholarly articles from the journal:http://www.tandf.co.uk/journals/alphalist.asp. Contact: The American Center for the Study of Distance Education, The Pennsylvania State University, College of Education, 411 Keller Building, University Park, PA 16802-3202; 814-863-3764

Center for Research on Teaching and Learning, maintained by the University of Michigan, includes links to articles on teaching strategies, many related to distance education: http://www.crlt.umich.edu/

Chronicle of Higher Education: **Information Technology,** the education newspaper's IT section: http://chronicle.com/infotech/

Distance Education Clearinghouse from the University of Wisconsin, a good one-stop resource for information about distance education: http://www.uwex.edu/disted/

Distance-Educator.com, with reports available through the Distance EdeZine link: http://www.distance-educator.com/

Educational Technology, Research and Development, a journal of research on educational technology at all levels: http://www.aect.org/Intranet/Publications/index.asp. Contact: Association for Educational Communications and Technology, 1800 N. Stonelake Dr. Suite 2, Bloomington, IN 47404; 877-677-AECT or 812-335-7675

Encyclopedia of Educational Technology, a collection of short articles both practical and theoretical: http://coe.sdsu.edu/eet/

Institute for Learning Technologies, a list of projects under way in distance education: http://www.ilt.columbia.edu/projects/index.html

Interpersonal Computing and Technology Journal, a peer-reviewed journal focused on computer-mediated communication in education: http://www.aect.org/Intranet/Publications/index.asp. Contact: Association for Educational Communications and Technology, 1800 North Stonelake Drive, Suite 2, Bloomington, IN 47404; 877.677.AECT or 812.335.7675

Instructional Technology Council, a site with links to research and awards related to distance education, as well as directories of learning object repositories and online courses: http://www.itcnetwork.org/

Journal of Asynchronous Learning Networks focuses on research in online learning: http://www.sloan-c.org/publications/jaln/. Contact: JALN, The Sloan Center at Olin and Babson Colleges, Franklin W. Olin College of Engineering, Olin Way, Needham, MA 02492-1200; 781-292-2523

Journal of Interactive Online Learning, a peer-reviewed journal full of excellent research articles on distance education: http://www.ncolr. org/jiol/issues/. Contact: JIOL, The University of Alabama, Tuscaloosa, AL 35487; 205-348-7010

Journal of Computer-Mediated Communication, an online journal from the University of Southern California that deals with online communication in general, with some articles focused on education: http://www.blackwell-synergy.com/loi/jcmc. Contact: JCMC, School of Library and Information Science, Indiana University, 1320 E. 10th Street L1 011, Bloomington, IN 47405-3907; 812-855-2018.

Learning Technology, a newsletter published by the Institute of Electrical and Electronics Engineers Computer Society Technical Committee on Learning Technology: http://lttf.ieee.org/learn_tech/index.html. Contact: IEEE, 1730 Massachusetts Avenue, N.W., Washington, DC 20036-1992; 1-202-371-0101

T.H.E. Journal: Technological Horizons in Education, a magazine with a heavy emphasis on the technology: http://www.thejournal.com/ Contact: 17501 17th St., Suite 230, Tustin, CA 92780; 714-730-4011

United States Distance Learning Association, with a link to archives of the *USDLA Journal*: http://www.usdla.org/

Listservs and other discussion forums

Sharing experiences and concerns is easy through online discussion forums, with listservs delivered through e-mail the most common structure. Here are some gatherings you may want to check out:

Adjunctnation.com, a collection of articles along with a user blog: http://www.AdjunctNation.com/other/blog/login

Distance Education Online Symposium, from the American Center for the Study of Distance Education at Penn State, including both DEOSNEWS, an electronic journal for distance educators, and DEOS-L, a moderated electronic forum: http://www.ed.psu.edu/acsde/deos/deos.asp

Diversity University, a real-time Internet accessible virtual reality educational environment that was the first MOO (Multi-user dimension, Object-Oriented communication forum) designed for classroom use: http://www.du.org/

EDTECH Discussion List, a moderated listserv focused on educational technology and sponsored by H-NET Humanities Online: http://www.h-net.org/~edweb/list.html

EDUPAGE, a listserv about information technology: http://www.educause.edu/content.asp?page_id=639&bhcp=1

Media in Education, a listserv: http://listserv.binghamton.edu/cgi-bin/wa.exe?A0=MEDIA-L

Online Chronicle of Distance Education and Communication, a listserv and e-mail bulletin maintained by Nova Southeastern University: http://tecfa.unige.ch/tecfa/teaching/staf17/backup/9899/fabrice/staf17-disted.html

TLT-SWG, a moderated listserv about improving teaching and learning with a focus on the role of technology in higher education: http://www.tltgroup.org/tlt-swg.htm

Web Based Training/Online Learning Listserv, focused on the development of Web-based training and e-learning programs: http://www.trainingplace.com/source/thelist.html

Conferences

Some colleges offer travel funds for adjuncts, so investigate that possibility. Here are some of the better known conferences related to distance education:

Angel User Conference: http://angelconference.medicine.iu.edu/

Annual Conference on Distance Teaching & Learning: http://www.uwex.edu/disted/conference/

Association for Educational Communications and Technology Conference: http://www.aect.org/Events/

Blackboard Users Conference: http://www.blackboard.com/company/events/

Canadian Network for Innovation in Education (CNIE) Conference: http://www.athabascau.ca/CNIE-RCIE/english/index.php

CITE Conference: http://cite.ecollege.com/

Conference on College Teaching and Learning: http://www.teachlearn.org/

Conference on Information Technology: http://www.league.org/league/partners/confer_profile.htm#cit

E-Learn: http://www.aace.org/conf/eLearn/default.htm

E-Learning: http://www.itcnetwork.org

ED-MEDIA Educational Technology Conference: http://www.aace.org/conf/edmedia/

MERLOT International Conference: http://conference.merlot.org/

Microcomputers in Education Conference: http://mec.asu.edu/

The National Educational Computing Conference: http://center.uoregon.edu/ISTE/NECC2008/

Sloan-C International Conference on Asynchronous Learning Networks: http://www.sloan-c.org/conference/index.asp

Society for Information Technology and Teacher Education:
http://www.aace.org/conf/site/

Teaching and Learning with Technology Conference:
http://www.itap.purdue.edu/tlt/conference/

TechEd International Conference and Exposition:
http://www.techedevents.org

Texas Distance Learning Association Conferences:
http://www.txdla.org/conference/2008/

United States Distance Learning Association Conferences:
http://www.usdla.org/html/events/conferences.htm

WebCT Users Conference: http://webct.confex.com/webct/2006/
techprogram/MEETING.HTM

e-Learning Blogs

From learning theories to content design, metadata to LMSes,
survey data to industry trends, these blogs have it all:

Digital Chalkie:
http://www.digitalchalkie.com/
The main purpose of Digital Chalkie is to provide an open hub for Oceania
educators using ICT to engage in dialogue that may help facilitate the best
educational outcomes for their students.

Digital Writing, Digital Teaching:
http://hickstro.org/
Digital Writing, Digital Teaching is a blog written by Troy Hicks, an assis-
tant professor of English at Central Michigan University and a Co-Director
for the Red Cedar Writing Project. Named one of the top 100 educational
blogs by OEDb, It explores the variety of issues related to teaching writing
with new media for K-12 teachers and teacher educators.

elearningpost:
http://www.elearningpost.com/
Daily headlines.
E-Learning Queen:
http://elearnqueen.blogspot.com/
E-Learning Queen focuses on distance training and education, from in-

structional design to e-learning and mobile solutions, and pays attention to psychological, social, and cultural factors. The edublog emphasizes real-world e-learning issues and appropriate uses of emerging technologies.

George Siemens' elearnspace:
http://www.elearnspace.org/blog/
This blog and its encompassing site "explore elearning, knowledge management, networks, technology, and community."

Harold Jarche:
http://www.jarche.com/
A blog about "conversations at the intersection of learning, work & technology." Take a look at his recent entry on the system he uses for Personal Knowledge Management in a Web 2.0 world.

Internet Time Blog:
http://internettime.com/
Well-known for his theories on informal learning, this is Jay Cross's original blog, where he explores all facets of learning and technology.

Online Learning Update:
http://people.uis.edu/rschr1/onlinelearning/blogger.html
Like the elearningpost, but focused more on academia.

Robin Good's MasterViews International:
http://masterview.ikonosnewmedia.com/
From the online media expert himself, this blog is focused on PowerPoint and presentation skills. (Robin once called Articulate Presenter "the Ferrari of rich-media Web presentation tools.")

The Rapid eLearning Blog:
http://www.articulate.com/rapid-elearning/
Tom Kuhlmann blogs regularly at The Rapid eLearning Blog, which has nearly 10,000 subscribers, making it the most read blog in the elearning industry.

Tony Karrer's eLearning Technology:
http://elearningtech.blogspot.com/2006/08/first-time-visitor-guide.html
Be sure to see his First Time Visitor Guide, which highlights some of Tony's previous posts on topics ranging from Elearning 2.0 to informal learning to Learning Management Systems.

XplanaZine:
http://www.xplanazine.com
XplanaZine editors are dedicated to bringing you news and expert opinions in the areas of publishing and pedagogy. We search the Web for the most recent news about publishing companies, information technology, online education research, and schools and programs implementing new methods to educate students.

Awards

The following awards in the area of distance education are open to adjunct instructors. Some come with cash awards; others offer recognition that can help advance your career:

American Association of Community Colleges: The $5,000 David R. Pierce Faculty Technology Award is given to a full- or part-time faculty member (nominated by the institution) at a community college who excels in the use of information technology in teaching. Information: http://www.aacc.nche.edu/Content/NavigationMenu/AboutAACC/Awards/Awards.htm

Instructional Technology Council: Colleges are invited to submit nominations for Outstanding Online Faculty, with two awards given annually. Information: http://www.itcnetwork.org/

MERLOT: Faculty of all ranks are invited to submit lesson plans for peer review on MERLOT, and they are also invited to apply to become peer reviewers in their area of expertise. Faculty can also submit material for consideration for an award for "exemplary online learning resources" that includes $500 cash, a $1000 travel stipend, and free conference registration to MERLOT's annual international conference. Information: http://www.merlot.org/merlot/index.htm.

National Education Association: Three $2500 Excellence in the Academy awards (plus travel expenses to the annual convention) are given to full- or part-time faculty members each year for essays about teaching, which have included those about teaching online. Information: http://www2.nea.org/he/ajeaward.html.

Sloan Consortium: This organization gives a $2,000 award (based on institutional nomination) for outstanding online teaching. Information: http://www.aln.org/awards/index.asp. An award is also given for effective practices. Information: http://www.aln.org/awards/epcall.asp

U.S. Distance Learning Association: This organization gives an annual award for Excellence in Distance Learning Teaching. Nomination is required, and there is a $100 entry fee. Information: http://www.usdla.org/html/events/dlAwards.htm

WebCT: This course management system annually recognizes exemplary courses that use its course management system. Information: http://www.webct.com/exemplary

SAMPLE COURSE DEVELOPMENT CONTRACT

XYZ University Course Development Contract

Annie Adjunct will receive $1000 to develop for XYZ University online course Math 110.

Training:
Annie Adjunct is required to attend faculty training sessions on any two of the following topics: Online Course Design, Managing Online Students, Using Online Communication Tools.

Deadlines:
A syllabus is due to the distance education coordinator by November 15, 2005. The finished course must be ready for evaluation by March 15, 2006. All revisions to the course must be completed by April 15, 2006. The course will be offered beginning in the 2006 summer semester.

Description:
The following are required elements of every online course at XYZ University:
Syllabus
Course objectives
Content modules
Detailed assignment descriptions
Lectures (one per module)
Plan for the use of discussion boards
Ownership:
XYZ University will hold copyright to all original course materials developed under this agreement, and no royalty or residual payments will be due to Annie Adjunct for the use of these materials.

Reviewed and approved by:

Faculty member signature:

Date:

REFERENCES

Angelo, T., & Cross, P. K. *Classroom assessment techniques: A handbook for college teachers* (2nd ed.). San Francisco: Jossey-Bass, 1993.

Bonk, C. J., Wisher, R. A., & Lee, J. "Moderating learner-centered e-learning problems and solutions, benefits and implications." In T. S. Roberts (Ed.). *Online collaborative learning: Theory and practice* (pp. 54-85). Hershey, Pa.: Idea Group, 2003.

Bramucci, R. (2001). "Ideas for distance learning." Retrieved September 11, 2004 from the World Wide Web: <http://fdc.fullerton.edu/learning/STG2001_IDEAS.htm>.

Gardner, H. *Multiple intelligences: The theory in practice*. NewYork: Basic Books, 1993.

Greive, Donald. *A Handbook for Adjunct/Part-Time Faculty and Teachers of Adults* (6th ed.). Ann Arbor: Part-time Press, Inc, 2006.

Lazarus, B. D. "Teaching courses online: How much time does it take?" *Journal of asynchronous learning networks*,7(3). Retrieved November 9, 2004 from the World Wide Web: <http://www.sloan-c.org/publications/jaln/v7n3/v7n3_lazarus.asp>.

Moore, M. G., & Anderson, W. G. (Eds.). *Handbook of distance education*. Mahwah, N.J.: Lawrence Erlbaum, 2003.

Muilenburg, Lin, & Berge, Z. L. "A framework for designing questions for online learning." Retrieved September 2, 2004 from the World Wide Web: <http://www.emoderators.com/moderators/muilenburg.html>.

Neuhauser, C. "A maturity model: Does it provide a path for online course design?" *Journal of interactive online learning*, 3(1). Retrieved August 30, 2004 from the World Wide Web: <http://www.ncolr.org/jiol/issues/>.

"A profile of participation in distance education: 1999-2000." National Center for Education Statistics. Retrieved November 9, 2004 from the World Wide Web: <http://nces.ed.gov/pubs2003/2003154.pdf>.

Palloff, R. M., & Pratt, K. *Building learning communities in cyberspace: Effective strategies for the online classroom*. San Francisco: Jossey-Bass, 1999.

Palloff, R. M., & Pratt, K. *The virtual student: A profile and guide to working with online learners*. San Francisco: Jossey-Bass, 2003.

Parker, A. "Identifying predictors of academic persistence in distance education." *USDLA Journal,17(1)*. Retrieved November 9, 2004 from the World Wide Web: <http://www.usdla.org/html/journal/JAN03_Issue/article06.html>.

"Quality on the line: Benchmarks for success in Internet-based distance education." The Institute for Higher Education Policy. Retrieved August 30, 2004 from the World Wide Web: <http://www.ihep.com/Pubs/PDF/Quality.pdf>.

Prensky, M. *Digital game-based learning*. New York: McGraw-Hill, 2001.

Russell, T. L. *The no significant difference phenomenon*. Raleigh, N.C.: North Carolina State University, 1999.

The Sloan Consortium. "Entering the mainstream: the quality and extent of online education in the United States, 2003 and 2004." Retrieved March 3, 2005 from the World Wide Web: <http://www.sloan-c.org/resources/entering_mainstream.pdf>.

The Sloan Consortium. "Sizing the opportunity: The quality and extent of online education in the United States, 2002 and 2003." Retrieved August 30, 2004 from the World Wide Web: <http://www.sloan-c.org/resources/sizing_opportunity.pdf>.

Spatariu, A., Hartley, K., & Bendixen, L. D. "Defining and measuring quality in online discussions." *Journal of Interactive Online Learning*, 2(4). Retrieved August 30, 2004 from the World Wide Web: <http://www.ncolr.org/jiol/issues/showissue.cfm?volID=2&IssueID=9>.

Sunal, D. W., Sunal, C. S., Odell, M.R., & Sundberg, C. A. "Research-supported best practices for developing online learning." *Journal of Interactive Online Learning*, 2(1). Retrieved August 30, 2004 from the World Wide Web: <http://www.ncolr.org/jiol/issues/showissue.cfm?volID=2&IssueID=6>.

Wang, A. Y., & Newlin, M. H. "Online lectures: Benefits for the virtual classroom." *T.H.E. Journal Online*. Aug. 2001. Retrieved September 2, 2004 from the World Wide Web: <http://www.thejournal.com/articles/15513>.

Wheeler, Gary S. *Teaching and Learning in College* (4th ed.). Ann Arbor: The Part-Time Press, Inc., 2003.

Zimmerman, B. J. "Self-regulated learning and academic achievement: An overview." *Educational Psychologist*, 25 (1990): 3-17.

Index

group tests 26
guest experts 8, 60, 61

H

Hartley, K. 89
Home Page. *See also* URL
host 13
HTML 10, 13, 45, 46
HTTP 13
humor 51, 54
hybrid courses 3-4
hypertext 13
Hyper Text Markup Language. *See* HTML
Hypertext Transfer Protocol. *See* HTTP

I

icebreaker 50
IM 30
Instant Messaging 30. *See* IM
Institute for Higher Education Policy 47
Instructional Television Fixed Service. *See* ITFS
Integrated Services Digital Network. *See* IDSN
interactive media 13
interactivity 20
international accessibility guidelines 45. *See also* Bobby
Internet 61, 62
Internet Service Provider 18. *See also* ISP
ISDN 13
ISP 10, 18-19, 29
ITFS 13

J

Journal of Interactive and Online Learning 20
J. Sargent Reynolds Community College 23
Juno (ISP) 19. *See also* ISP
Justice Department Reauthorization Act 40. *See also* copyright

K

Kaplan College 59
Kobler, Linda 51-52

O

O'Connor, Thomas 52
Odell, M.R, 89
Odell, M.R. 89
online 14
online classrooms 19
Online Course Design Maturity Model 20
online projects 68. *See also* group projects
origination site 14

P

Palloff, R. M. 88
Paradise Valley Community College 62
Parker, Angie 47, 89
Patel, Amar 53
PBL. *See* problem-based learning
peer review 20, 69
Pennsylvania State University 46
Piedmont Technical College 49
plagiarism 7, 25, 26, 34
Point of Presence. *See* POP
point-to-multipoint 14
point-to-point 14
POP 14
PowerPoint 37, 44-46, 67, 69, 81
PPP 14
Pratt, K. 88
Prensky, M. 67, 89
presentations 53, 69, 71
problem-based learning 8, 65
protocol 14

Q

QuickTime 54. *See also* streaming media

R

Raiford, Norman 52
Randolph Community College 3
real-time data 61, 62
recipe assignments 27
Rehabilitation Act 45. *See also* accessibility
research 47, 76, 89

tests 3, 26, 27, 71
The National Center for Case Study Teaching in Science 65
The Sloan Consortium 89
threaded discussion 61. *See also* discussions
Transmission Control Protocol. *See* TCP
transponder 15

U

Uniform Resource Locator. *See* URL
University of Illinois at Urbana-Champaign 53
University of Massachusetts at Lowell 66
University of Michigan-Dearborn 19
University of Minnesota 66
University of Mississippi 20
University of Wisconsin 20
University of Wisconsin-Madison 53
University of Wisconsin Stevens Point 20
uplink 15
URL 10, 13, 15

V

Vault.com 4, 5
video lectures 8, 53, 54
video Teleconferencing 15
Virginia Community College System 51
virus protection 18. *See also* McAfee

W

Wang, A. Y. 89
Waubonsee Community College 19
WebCT 19, 20, 33, 35, 83, 85
Weber State University 20
web log 31. *See also* blogs
West Virginia Community College 69
Wheeler, Gary S. 89
Williams College 67
Windows Media 54. *See also* streaming media
Wisher, R. A. 69, 88
World Lecture Hall 42
World Wide Web. *See* WWW
writing assignments 65
WWW 15

Y

Z

Part-Time Press, Inc. Instructional Products

Qty	Title	Unit $$

Total

Handbook for Adjunct/Part-Time Faculty	(paperback) $16.00
Handbook II: Advanced Teaching Strategies	(paperback) $17.00
Teaching and Learning in College	(paperback) $20.00
Managing Adjunct/Part-Time Faculty	(paperback) $25.00
Teaching Strategies and Techniques	(paperback) $10.00
Going the Distance: A Handbook	(paperback) $13.00

Adjunct Advocate: An Online Journal for Adjunct Faculty

(1-yr. subscription) $20.00

☐ *Check (payable to The Part-Time Press)*

☐ *Credit Card #* _____

*Exp. Date*_____ *CCV Code*_____

☐ *Purchase Order #*_____

Name _____

Institution _____

Address _____

City/ST/Zip _____

Phone: _____

FAX: _____

E-mail: _____

Shipping and Handling Fee Schedule: *8% of purchase subtotal*

Send to: Part-Time Press, P.O. Box 130117, Ann Arbor, MI 48113-0117; Fax to: 734-665-9001; Phone 734-930-6854 Order online: Part-TimePress.com

Date Due

BRODART, CO.   Cat. No. 23-233   Printed in U.S.A.